*Ayo Gurkha!*

J. M. MARKS

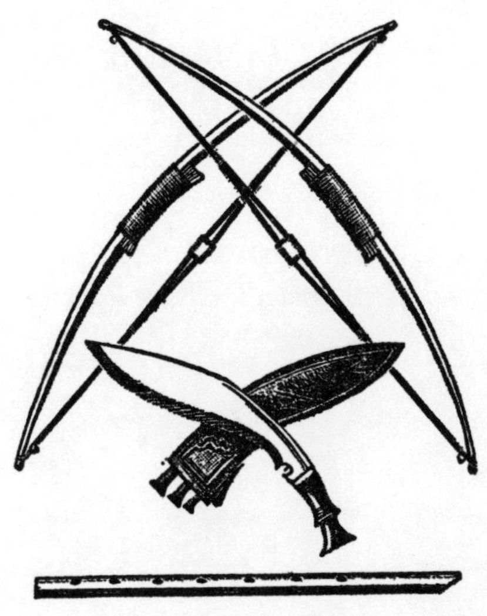

# *Ayo Gurkha!*

*Illustrated by*
GORAY DOUGLAS

*London*
OXFORD UNIVERSITY PRESS
*1971*

*Oxford University Press, Ely House, London W.1*
GLASGOW NEW YORK TORONTO MELBOURNE WELLINGTON
CAPE TOWN SALISBURY IBADAN NAIROBI DAR ES SALAAM LUSAKA ADDIS ABABA
BOMBAY CALCUTTA MADRAS KARACHI LAHORE DACCA
KUALA LUMPUR SINGAPORE HONG KONG TOKYO


First published 1971

*Maps drawn by Bruce Roberts*

*Printed in Great Britain by*
*Western Printing Services Ltd, Bristol*

# Contents

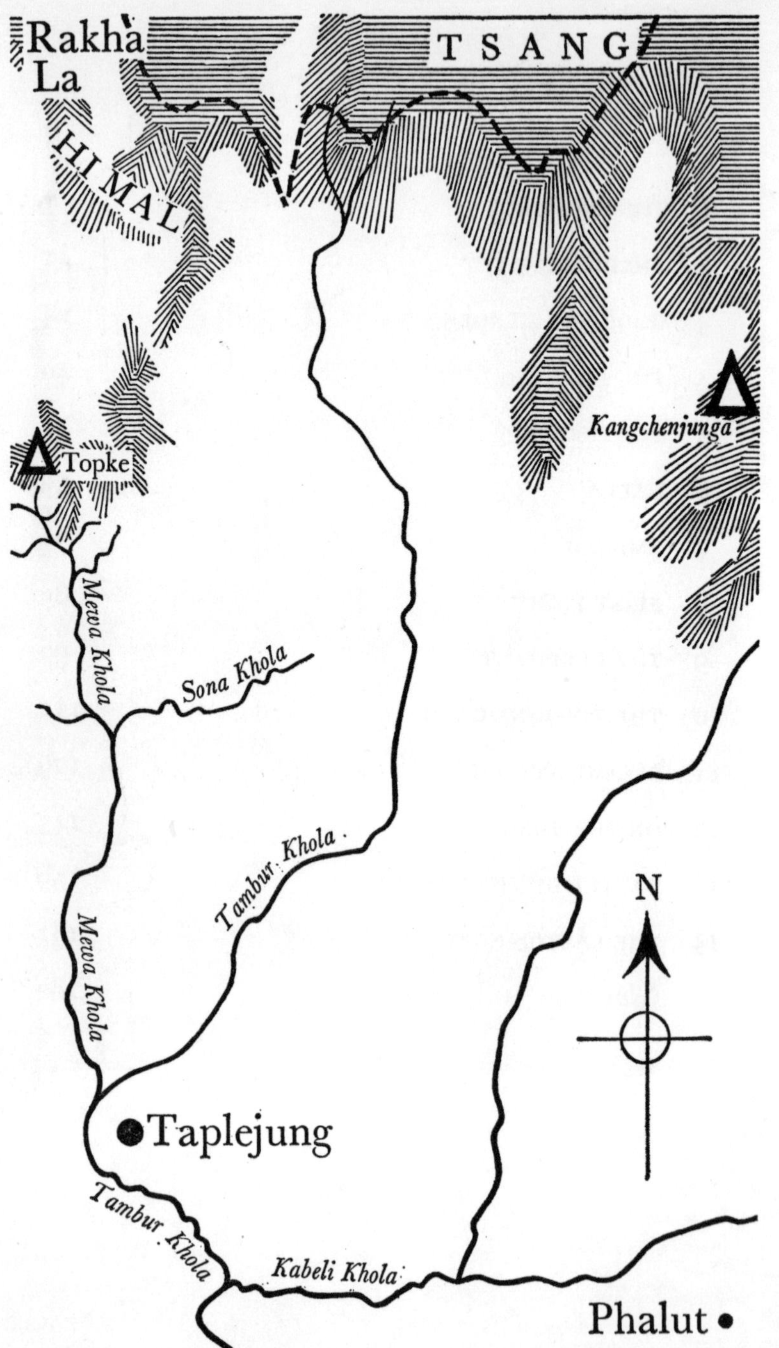
Rakha La
TSANG
HIMAL
Topke
Kangchenjunga
Mewa Khola
Sona Khola
Tambur Khola
Mewa Khola
N
Taplejung
Tambur Khola
Kabeli Khola
Phalut

sometimes playing with his elder brother Balahang and later with a little sister, Maya, and often with another little boy a few months older than himself, Manbahadur, a son of their neighbours. It was a peaceful time for Aitahang, for he was not yet old enough to understand when talk of a new war with the Germans spread through the Gurkha hills. More important to him were the immediate incidents of life in their remote valley—the birth of a new calf, chicks hatching, the great water-buffaloes passing ponderously at ploughing time, his father setting off for the autumn bazaar at Taplejung with a load of produce on his back; occasionally a traveller asking for a night's shelter. Even the eventual news of the war ending meant little to him, though he remembered his parents talking sadly of young men who would not return.

He was seven years old and his childhood was ending when the first really memorable incident of his life occurred and he received his first and—so he thought all his life—his finest gift.

This gift was the pelt of a bear, a great bearskin rug into which he snuggled at night. He loved the warm fur, for the wind blowing into the Gurkha hills from Tibet brought the icy breath of glaciers with it. But he also loved the fur because his father had killed the bear himself—a big black Himalayan bear in a savage mood found looting their winter stores of corn-cobs, who just would not be frightened off with shouts and volleys of stones. The leathery skin had stiffened in places and the thick hair felt scratchy against his bare legs—but how warm it was! He was sure that it was warmer than the sheepskins and woollen blankets in which his parents huddled beside him, his baby sister between them. The only cosier place, he admitted secretly, was the hayloft above the cattle in the byre, where Elder Brother slept. But he, Aitahang, would not sleep there until he was of an age to do proper boy's work—herding cattle in the low field and sheep and goats on the high mountain pasture. He would be old enough, though, when this winter passed and he entered his eighth year; already his brother Balahang was an experienced shepherd—after all, he was eleven years old.

Yes, Aitahang remembered the day of the bear, when his brother came racing downhill to where his father sat slicing binding strips from a section of green bamboo. 'Bear,' he panted, 'at the corn store—' At once Aitahang was swept up by his mother into the house, but from the door he saw his father jump up, replace his kukri in its scabbard and hurry uphill to the corn store under its thatched roof, shouting and clapping his hands. 'Hey, *sala jata, chhori deu, ja!*' he shouted in Gurkhali, while Elder Brother gathered stones and flung them into the store. But in a few minutes they came running back. 'Quick,' commanded his father, 'the gun!'

Aitahang remembered his mother's clutch of alarm, but she left him at once to snatch down the old single-barrelled muzzle-loader from its nail inside the door and hand it out.

'A villain, this one,' his father grunted as he rammed down charge, ball and wadding and set the firing cap before hurrying uphill again. 'Keep back, son,' he called. Elder Brother backed away from the store and as his father circled warily Aitahang heard the invisible bear's growls, warning them to keep away while he plundered. Then came an enormous flash-bang, a cloud of smoke, the smell of burnt powder and frantic snarling roars, and the bear came tumbling and pawing into the open, biting at the wound in his body—badly hit, but still alive and very dangerous. He looked round, small eyes glowing with rage and teeth and muzzle foaming and bloody, saw the man and boy and started scrabbling his way towards them.

'Axe!' his father shouted. 'The axe—quick!' He was backing away, eyes on the bear. There was no time to reload and he knew that if he moved too quickly the bear would turn on whoever was nearest, possibly the boy Aitahang watching from the doorway beside his mother. The axe lay by the stack of firewood, a few yards behind the house and up towards the bear. His mother did not hesitate. She ran up, picked up the axe and threw it right over the bear to land by the man on the far side. He snatched it up as the bear lurched to its hind legs to get him, swung it high and smashed it down on the bear's skull. The heavy animal crashed forward, knocking the man over in its fall; he struggled out from beneath it, and Aitahang remembered how white lines stood out through his father's torn sleeve, then turned to red as blood dripped down his arm. His mother screamed but his father laughed: 'He's dead. But,' he added, looking down at his arm, 'he had sharp claws!'

As soon as his father's claw wounds had been bound up the whole family set about restoring order to the looted corn store—picking up and stacking the cobs still in their leafy covers and putting aside thriftily those that had been partially gnawed by the bear—they would do for the hens, and would not be wasted.

Then they set about dealing with the carcass of the bear itself. Father and Elder Brother removed the pelt, using sharp little skinning knives carried in the back of the kukri scabbard. Very carefully they removed and set aside the claws, muzzle-whiskers and teeth. 'The Tibetan traders'll give us a good ten rupees for those,' commented Padamlal, as Mother wrapped them in a square of cloth and stowed them away up on one of the beams of the veranda. 'They'll use 'em for medicine, or for magic—great magicians, these Tibetans!'

The others nodded. They saw the wandering Tibetan traders every year, when they came across from Tsang Province through the high Pass of Rakha, or farther east through the pass above Walunchung Gola. They felt no strangeness with these Tibetans, for they themselves, according to tradition, were the descendents of Tibetan yak-herds from Tsang. But two particularly fine eye-teeth—great white fangs, they were—Padamlal cleaned carefully and inserted into the necklace amulets of his two young sons. 'There,' he said, 'they will bring you strength in times of stress.'

But ten rupees—that was more money than the household saw in a month. 'Do you think they'll give us as much as ten, Father?' asked Balahang.

'Yes, I do,' his father replied, while Aitahang stroked the dark fur and looked with awe at the heavy jaws. 'This fellow's a big male, strong and dangerous. It isn't often they get a chance of medicine from such a powerful beast. Yes—ten rupees at least! And if they won't buy, why, I'll see what our own Limbu medicine-men will give us when we go down to the spring fair at Taplejung!' He looked across at Aitahang with a smile. 'D'you like it, Second Son? Well, you shall have it. You need a blanket of your very own, and Elder Son is warm enough in the hayloft already, and has a good blanket of his own. As soon as we've cleaned and cured this pelt you can keep it!'

Aitahang had never had such a gift before. He was overwhelmed, and could only sit looking at his parents and stroking the still-warm fur, while his heart swelled with pride of ownership till he felt he might burst.

That afternoon his father and his elder brother made a framework of saplings and stretched out the pelt on it, scraping the underside clean and then rubbing into it a mixture of salt and powder his father ground from an outcrop of yellowish rock. Then they exposed the pelt to the winter sun and wind and left it there for day after day to dry, occasionally tightening the thongs that held it taut, and every day Aitahang went out to look at it and see if it were ready, till the great day came when it was unloosed from the frame and his father handed it to him. That night he was almost too excited to sleep, for not only was he wrapped in his own fur blanket but his father had told him that when the first warming gleams of spring arrived he would join his brother to work—no longer a child about the house, but a real boy.

Earlier he had asked: 'Father, what did you say to the bear?'

His father laughed. 'Oh, I only called him rude names and told him to clear off!'

'Can you speak bear's language?'

'No, child—' His father laughed again. 'I spoke in the mountain tongue, Gurkhali, which you will learn soon, so that you can speak with other clans. I did not use our Limbu language, for the bear isn't one of us, and wouldn't understand.'

That seemed logical enough, and it explained one of the puzzles of his childhood: why his father sometimes passed the time of day with travellers with strange words Aitahang did not understand.

At night he slept more soundly than ever in his new furry covering, and it was with surprise one morning near the end of winter that he woke to find Balahang sleeping with them in the farm-house. He then remembered something disturbing his parents during the night, their alarmed whispers of 'Sokpa!', his brother being fetched hurriedly from the hay-loft, and outside in the dark, echoing down from the frozen slopes, a high, whistling cry. 'Why is Elder Brother here?' he asked. 'What happened last night?' But his parents evaded his question, and soon he forgot.

The winter passed and Aitahang began learning to graze the cattle. He had been used to them since he could toddle, and they in turn had become used to him, so they were not startled when he took them off to graze after ploughing. They knew the way better than he did, and paid little attention beyond swishing their tails at him as he trotted behind them in his bare feet, white jodhpurs and ragged cotton tunic flapping in the wind.

With the warmer weather the snow-line on the high pastures shrank back till it reached the stretches of high dark forests, the snow lying under the trees a few more weeks, the drifts turning greyer and smaller till at last they retreated altogether to the permanent snow-line of the Himal. Then came the Tibetans.

The first to arrive was a very tall, shaven-headed monk in red robe and felt boots, appearing round the shoulder of a hill in the chill of evening. On his back he carried a frame support of thick cane on which was bound a pack holding his belongings. As he approached Padamlal noted the look of authority about him, though when he came near he bowed his head in greeting, politely lowering his eyes. He produced a bowl of carved and polished wood, dark and silk-smooth with use, and held it out, and at once Aitahang's mother, Ama, fetched food for him, maize porridge first, with water in a metal cup to drink.

Before eating, the monk took off his pack and swung it down, and from the fold of robe above his tight sash he took out a small lively bundle of silky fur with bright suspicious eyes and sharp white teeth.

'A dog!' Aitahang gazed at it in wonder. He had never seen such a dog before. The monk smiled. 'Apso,' he said. 'Lhasa Apso!' and placed the little dog on top of his pack, where it settled itself importantly.

Aitahang was fascinated, and Padamlal explained: 'These little dogs are the guardians of their master's belongings. This breed have been doing this for hundreds of years, and the puppies now do not need training, they do this instinctively.' He nodded at it. 'They are valuable. The monks breed them in certain monasteries, and only part with them to senior monks or to noble Tibetans.' He saw a longing look in Aitahang's eyes and shook his head with a smile. 'Even if we could get one it would be no use to us here, my son. These hills are dangerous for little dogs, and this fellow's long hair would be a terrible hindrance in the rainy season in mid-summer. Tibet's fine and dry for them, but the Gurkha hills are a different matter.' He smiled ruefully. 'One of those big ones that the Tibetans have would be useful, but they're not cheap!'

That night the monk slept by the fire in the lower room of the farm-house. Apart from muttered prayers he had hardly spoken a word.

Early the next morning the monk made ready to leave, but after he had eaten he spoke to Padamlal in a rough mixture of Gurkhali and Tibetan. With its many words common to the Limbus, this was quite well understood. 'For your hospitality,' he said, 'I have this morning said prayers for your household, but now, before I go, I will chart an oracle for your two sons,' and he seated himself on the veranda's earthen floor, and indicated that Balahang should sit before him. Then he took from his pack and opened out a heavily creased and faded chart nearly a yard across, drawn with signs and markings of the most intricate character. The Limbus stared at the chart uneasily. To them it smacked of the occult, of the powerful forces they knew lived in the forests and the glaciers, and inhabited the upper air. And these Tibetan monks . . . However, when the monk asked for the exact hour and date of Balahang's birth Padamlal supplied it readily. The monk noted it down with a flourish of his finger in the dust and, lips moving in a soundless murmer, studied the chart before him. Eventually he nodded his head and said, 'Your lucky number is five, but the number eleven holds no fortune for you. The colour yellow is favourable, but blue is not.'

Then he asked for some personal belonging of Balahang's and, after a slight hesitation, the lad twisted his kukri and scabbard from his cummerbund and handed them to him. Taking them in both hands the monk closed his eyes and sat very still and silent, almost as though he had gone to sleep, though watching curiously Padamlal saw beads of sweat break out on the broad forehead. Then the monk drew a deep breath, relaxed his tense posture and opened his eyes. He said: 'Broken water below a bridge is dangerous, but a bamboo grove offers deliverance.'

To the listening Limbus, noting every word, the advice on numbers and colours was not unfamiliar; it was perfectly logical that different persons would do better when omens and conditions were suitable and worse when they were unfavourable. It was all the more welcome to have these identified for them by a holy man, and a Tibetan at that. The other advice, however, seemed superfluous; all hill people knew that broken water meant rapids among rocks and was always dangerous—especially as so few Gurkhas could swim. The phrase about the bamboo grove seemed meaningless. But now it was Aitahang's turn.

He sat upright, his heels tucked beneath him in the posture of a Buddha, and watched the monk gravely. Again the monk scribbled flourishes in the dust, consulted his chart and studied the boy in front of him. Then he spoke: 'Thirteen is a number that will have great significance for you, and will eventually bring you fortune. The number four is not fortunate. For you yellow is neither favourable nor unfavourable, but must not be ignored. Red will bring advancement.'

The monk then asked for something personal of Aitahang's. At first this presented some difficulty, for the little boy had no kukri; he thought of the bear's fur, but that was bulky and anyway was upstairs in the farm-house, so he shyly removed and offered his little round skullcap with its frayed binding.

Again the monk sat still and silent, the little cap clasped tightly in his two hands. His face grew drawn and strained and once again the watchers saw sweat break out on his forehead. At length he relaxed, opened his eyes and breathed deeply. When he spoke it was more slowly, as if he knew that what he said must seem vague and meaningless. 'When you seek the One-Eyed,' he said, 'remember the leopard.'

The family stood in puzzled silence, waiting for some explanation of these cryptic words, but none was forthcoming. Instead, the monk glanced round at them with a compassionate expression, then rose to his feet, folded up his chart and put it away, and lifted the Apso terrier and stowed it away in his robe.

'Whither do you travel?' asked Padamlal as the monk fastened his pack. 'To the city of Katmandu?'

The monk shook his head and again Padamlal noticed the look of authority. 'I go to Lumbini in the Terai, the birthplace of our Lord Buddha.'

'And from which monastery do you come?'

'From Chhatreng, in Kham.'

'From Kham! You have come far!'

'I have walked for a year.'

The Tibetan swung up his pack, and as he adjusted the straps Padamlal caught a glimpse of colour beneath the neck of the robe, the corner of a yellow scarf, and he drew in his breath sharply. He knew something of these Tibetans, and this touch of yellow, together with the look of authority, told him that this was no common travelling monk. This was a Lama—a monk elevated by great learning, or one born to the yellow as a reincarnation. And here he was, on foot and alone, making his pilgrimage across the icy Himal and down through the Gurkha hills to Buddha's birthplace. The Lama sensed Padamlal's thoughts and silenced his unspoken question with a commanding glance. Then he murmured a benediction, turned and strode away downhill.

'I don't know what he meant by all that,' complained Ama, 'all that talk about leopards and bamboo groves and so on.' She was worried by the mysterious warnings, and tried to hide her fears in a display of irritation. 'Perhaps he wasn't a holy man at all!'

'He was a holy man, all right,' said Padamlal, half to himself, 'and we must remember what he said.' He stood in thoughtful silence for a moment, then looked round at the little group of his family, standing watching him expectantly, and laughed. 'I don't understand it either. But come now—back to work!'

He looked up at the snow-line. It was higher, and above it the sky was clean and blue. Spring was on its way.

## 2 SHEPHERD-BOY

'Your first day as a shepherd, Aitahang!' It was early dawn, very cold and the hill-sides were still in shadow. Dark night lingered in the deep gorges of the Mewa Khola, but in the enormous V of hill-side above, the snowy peak of Topke floated on its cushion of cloud—grey, then pink, then purest white. As his bare feet grew numb against the icy ground Aitahang momentarily regretted his warm sleeping-fur, but resolutely put it out of his mind. This was his first day as a real boy—he must put childish softness behind him.

He trotted along behind Balahang to the pen. 'First,' said Balahang hurriedly, 'we check to see that nothing's been taken in the night by a leopard or jackal.' In the growing light, they checked the hens and the goats and sheep in their pen. 'All correct,' hissed Balahang between chattering teeth. 'Come on, we'll take them up to the low pasture first.' He dragged back the log bars to the pen and the goats and sheep streamed past him. 'Lah! Lah!' he urged, and Aitahang trotted behind him, echoing 'Lah! Lah!' From the farm-house they could hear the bump of heavy shutters being taken down and smelt the first smoke of the fire being blown up from the embers of the day before. Not till mid-morning would their father bring them up a packet of food and a container of butter-milk to sustain them for the day. Like all other Gurkha clans the Limbus started the day with no more than a drink of water.

By the time it was broad daylight they were well up the sloping face of the low pasture and the animals were beginning to snatch at the short grass. Aitahang was happy enough to pause, for they were now a good five hundred feet up behind the house. The more extensive pastures were higher up, and he asked, 'Why are we stopping here?'

'The frost won't be off the grazing yet, and we'll wait here until the light in the woods is better.'

Aitahang looked at the dark, forested ridge above the open grassy pastures. Strange things lived in those woods; it was indeed better to wait.

As the sun warmed the earth the frozen rime disappeared from the blades of stiff grass and the boys set off uphill again with their flock. They soon warmed up and by the time they had reached the high pastures, now well over a thousand feet above the farm-house, Aitahang was warm and sweating, and panting a trifle, but he ignored this. His whole attention was concentrated on the flock, to see that none of its members strayed away.

'We'll keep them over to this patch today, Brother,' said Balahang, 'then tomorrow we'll graze them up and across a little —give the pasture a chance to recover by the time we work round to it again.' For a moment or two the boys were able to rest, and Aitahang wiped the sweat from his eyebrows. Balahang smiled wryly: 'Not too much time for sitting as a shepherd; there's always plenty to do, what with seeing the animals don't stray, keeping them from grazing too far uphill or downhill, tending to their troubles like burrs getting in their coats or thorns between their hoofs, examining sick-looking animals, and making sure that nothing is creeping up—or swooping down—to snatch off one of the lambs or kids.'

'What would attack them—jackals? leopards?'

'Well, there's the odd jackal about, though they usually hang around the Newar bazaars on the travel routes. Sometimes in good weather they'll come up in a pack to see what they can snatch. Leopards? I've never seen one, although they're in the hills all right. There's a bad one reported down across the Kabeli below Taplejung, but the only ones our father has ever warned me about are the snow-leopards. They eat mostly marmots in the high forest, and musk-deer. They don't bother us.' Balahang cocked an eye upwards and his gaze travelled across the sweep of sky above the tree-line, then he turned and studied the cliffs above the Mewa gorges below. Satisfied, he turned back to Aitahang and explained: 'Eagles,' he said. 'Black eagles, they're the things to watch, especially at lambing time. Sometimes they come down like a stone from the sky, sometimes up with a great rush from the gorge there, and unless we're quick they snatch up a lamb and they're off. Sometimes it's done so quickly and quietly you know nothing about it. They're cunning, and they go for the kids just out of sight of the shepherd, and then they fly off low behind rocks, or down into the gorge again, where they have their eyries in the rock face.'

All day they grazed the flock, and that evening, the animals safely penned and the evening meal eaten, Aitahang climbed upstairs, took his bundled-up sleeping fur and carried it down and across into the byre and stowed it up in the hayloft. This signified that he was a working boy at last, no longer a child sleeping with his parents. Returning to the house he thought he caught the ghost of a smile below his father's drooping moustaches—but no, he only seemed to be coughing a trifle over the fire.

It was dark a little after seven, and Aitahang was bone-weary from his long day in the steady winds of the high pasture. As soon as he had rinsed his mouth out and cleaned his teeth with the specially frayed twig of wood, he hurried to climb up into the hayloft and snuggle into his warm fur, then burying himself deep in the fragrant hay. Outside the rocks glittered in the moonlight as the frost closed down, harsh and silent.

'A night for the Sokpa,' murmured his brother as he huddled into his thick woollen rug beside him. 'The Himal is clear as day.'

'What's the Sokpa, Brother?' asked Aitahang drowsily, remembering vaguely his mother's warning 'Hush!' when his brother had mentioned it once before. But whether or not his brother made any answer he did not remember, for the next thing he knew it was grey dawn and he was being shaken awake again.

The next day seemed even harder than the first—possibly because he was still stiff from the first day's long climb up and the constant movement backwards and forwards watching the grazing animals. When he had a moment Aitahang gripped the little staff his father had cut for him and gazed fiercely about, looking for jackals to drive off, and into the sky to try and spot marauding eagles, but all was quiet and none appeared. Later, he was sure, he would have a kukri like the bigger boys, and then he would face anything—a bear, or even a leopard! Again that night he fell into a deep slumber as soon as he rolled himself in his fur. The third day, however, did not seem quite so hard, and he even began to recognize the various vantage points and landmarks scattered through the huge grazing area. With every day the weather grew a trifle warmer, and the snow-line shrank perceptibly.

'Soon will come the traders,' said Balahang knowledgeably, 'whenever the passes are clear of deep snow.' Aitahang wondered what they would bring: he had a strong feeling that they were bringing something specially for him.

It was a week later that the group of Tibetans arrived—half a dozen men in knee-length boots, woollen robes and fur hats, leading a string of half a dozen mules loaded with bundles and panniers. With them were also two women, striped aprons over their robes, their fur-trimmed hats decorated with patterned braid. These were the ones Padamlal had been waiting for, the traders. Along with them paced three very big dogs, shaggy and fierce-looking, one wearing a leather-studded collar. The two boys were up on the high pasture when they arrived, but Balahang sent Aitahang down. 'I'll stay with the flock; you go.' It was good of him, for visiting traders from Tibet were an event, something to remember and talk over—an incident in their hard lives.

When Aitahang reached the farm-house the Tibetans had

already opened one of their packs and were trying to interest his mother in buying medicines, speaking to her in a mixture of Tibetan and Gurkhali. 'Medicine for fever here, Ama-La, and this for easing headaches'—showing her small bundles of dried roots and herbs—'this for toothache and this for bleeding, and this one for pains in the joints . . .' So they went on persuasively, but although Ama looked at them with a mixture of caution and desire she shook her head firmly. She hesitated, though, to gaze irresolutely at one particularly strange-looking scrap of darkish leaf described as for infusions against chest pains. But it was to cost half a rupee—far more than they could afford. But 'Go on, Ama,' urged Padamlal with a grin, 'you get it.' Being a man he was a trifle sceptical of the value of some of the Tibetan medicines, whereas the women of the hills had implicit faith in their properties. So with a show of reluctance Ama untied her knotted money-scarf and bought the medicine with an Indian eight-anna piece.

'Now,' said Padamlal, '*I'll* sell them something!' and took down and opened the package with the bear claws and whiskers.

Aitahang watched the reaction of the traders with fascination. They kept their faces quite impassive, displaying no interest in the items whatsoever. At length Padamlal calmly began wrapping them up again, till a Tibetan put out a hand to restrain him. 'Bear?' he asked.

'Bear,' replied Padamlal.

'H'm—' The Tibetan raised an eyebrow. 'How much?'

'Ten rupees.'

At this the Tibetan seated by the medicine pack shook his head and said with a smile, '*Mangpo yu*—too much,' and went on, 'we will give medicines in exchange.' At this Padamlal also shook his head firmly and again began to gather up the valuable items. The Tibetan put out his hand again and hurriedly murmured a few words to the others. Aitahang began to see that they were anxious to secure the contents of the package, but equally they could not or would not part with money. But Padamlal equally wanted more than just medicines .

Again the Tibetans murmured, the seated man nodded, spoke a word or two and one of the group walked back to the mules, fumbled a moment in one of the great panniers and brought out a small, very shaggy puppy. He smiled and pointed to the puppy and then to the enormous mastiff with the studded leather collar —the puppy's father.

Now it was Padamlal's turn to mutter in Limbu Kura, 'Ama, we've always needed a watchdog.'

She was hesitant: 'It's not worth ten rupees—'

'It'll keep you safe when I'm away at market or when we're all out with the animals.'

Still Ama hesitated, and with a little smile the seated Tibetan took the puppy and passed it over to Aitahang. He held it in his arms, stroked its thick fur and scratched behind its ears. It licked his face and he turned to Padamlal: 'It looks just like a bear-cub, Father,' he said eagerly. 'We'll call it Bhalu—the Bear!'

The Tibetans relaxed and smiled and Padamlal sighed and handed over the package. So much for his hope of ten rupees! But secretly he was well pleased: these Tibetan mastiffs were strong and savage and very faithful. When that pup grew up no wandering robber would dare come near, and at night it would give warning of anything that approached, whether animal or man.

Their business done the Tibetans departed with courteous expressions of farewell, leaving Aitahang stroking the puppy on the veranda. At first it whined a little, but he brought it a bowlful of warm milk fresh from the cow, and it lapped and lapped till its little tummy expanded tight as a drum. 'There—you are a Limbu dog now!' declared Aitahang, and the puppy wagged its tail and went on lapping till at last it stopped, gave a final lick to the empty bowl, blinked in sleepy contentment, turned round once or twice on the veranda and settled down with a growling sigh beside the farm-house door.

'Look, Ama,' said Aitahang in delight, 'he is guarding us already!'

His father smiled agreement: 'He has the spirit of the bear in him, that one,' he said, then looked round and clapped his hands together, but softly, so as not to startle the new puppy: 'Back to work, now—back to work!' He looked up at the clear blue sky and sniffed the warm breeze from the south. Spring had arrived.

Day by day the two brothers grazed their flock up on the high pasture, a week passed, then another, spring softened into summer and one morning early Padamlal said to Aitahang, 'Now, Second Son, take the flock up on your own. There is more than enough other work for your elder brother to do.'

Aitahang was first astonished, then filled with a mixture of enormous pride and inner apprehension. How on earth would he manage, all alone up on the high pasture? And what if an eagle attacked, or even a leopard? But he nodded determinedly and at once ran to unbar the night pen and drive the flock uphill. Climbing up to the high pasture he was soon too busy to worry about anything other than his flock. In the weeks with Balahang he had learnt to recognize each and every one of them, and knew their identifying names—Big Black, Greystripes, Patch, Young Black and so on—even irreverent names like Elder Aunt or Third Cousin, from fancied resemblances to more distant members of the family.

His first day on the high pasture opened with an anxious few moments; he spotted a black eagle soaring above the rocks, but then he saw it glide round the upper cliff face and vanish, and realized that at this late stage in the year the kids and lambs were too heavy even for an eagle to carry off. That eagle was merely returning to its eyrie with smaller game, mice or voles, or possibly a marmot from up near the three frozen lakes.

Aitahang soon became accustomed to his solitary life high on the lonely pasture. One evening his friend Manbahadur showed him how to cut a slender cane and notch it into a flute, and he took it with him tucked into his cummerbund wherever he went. When he sat down for a moment he would take it out and pipe shrill notes, gazing over the backs of his flock right across the Mewa to the wild slopes beyond, dreaming of building a fine timber house there, with a dozen sons of his own to herd countless fat sheep. Sadly he blew a few notes: when he was grown and his father died he would share the land by the farm-house with his brother, and their sons would in turn sub-divide the land and so on, until each owned less than would feed a hen. 'Come on,' he urged the flock, springing up and putting his flute away. 'Come on up!' It was no use being gloomy—he was young, and would make his fortune somehow.

Then one day came tragedy. He looked down from his contemplation of the land across the Mewa, for instinct told him something was wrong, and quickly he counted the flock. His heart jumped, for there was one animal missing. He checked again, to find that the missing beast was one of their finest, the young male, Greystripes. Leaving the flock he tumbled and sprang downhill like a bouncing boulder till he was within calling distance of the farm-house and, pitching his voice high, called to Padamlal, then turned and raced back uphill to the flock.

'What is it?' Padamlal arrived panting.

'The grey goat's gone!'

'Off you go after him. Any idea which way?'

'No, but I'll try first above the gorge.'

'Be careful, son—keep a sharp lookout,' warned Padamlal as he settled himself to watch the flock.

Aitahang had often run to round up straying animals, but he had never so far had to search for one that had wandered out of sight. He would look for its slotted footprints, he decided, and began to look where he had last seen the animal grazing. This, he found, was easier said than done. When he examined the ground he saw slot marks everywhere, some obviously old, others freshly made, but in profusion. It seemed hopeless; he had no idea which were those of the lost goat. They all looked the same. In growing apprehension he cast out more widely, finding only unidentifiable slot prints, and in an hour he turned back, unhappy and miserable, to admit his failure.

Padamlal sighed: 'Never mind, Son,' and patted Aitahang to comfort him a little. 'It may come back by nightfall. It's impossible to keep them from straying sometimes.'

But Aitahang knew in himself that it was his fault in the end. First, he really had been dreaming, looking across the Mewa; second and perhaps more important, he had been unable to make any proper attempt at tracking it, as he didn't know how. Sitting alone with his flock in the sharp April wind he wept.

The grey goat did not reappear. Days later Aitahang came across tufts of grey hair in a dip in the hill-side only a few hundred yards from where he had discovered its loss. The ground seemed disturbed. He searched about, but could make nothing of the few, fading signs. Something had seized the goat and carried it off, but whether jackals or a leopard he could not tell.

It was at that moment, standing over the last few traces of the vanished goat, that Aitahang resolved that he would learn the secrets of tracking—how to read the language of the ground, and how to read it quickly. There was no one to train him; he must learn by himself. Filled with a burning determination he started there and then.

He began by following one of the larger goats as it grazed, to see if he could identify its prints a few moments later. Surely, he thought, that should be simple enough. But to his chagrin he found that even while watching the animal he found it difficult to separate its brand-new prints from those made earlier by other goats. But he persevered, and gradually found his eyes noticing the tiny differences between one print and another—variations in depth, irregularities in outline, individual marks left by horny hoofs scratched and frayed by rock. As he practised day after day he began to recognize the prints as being the signatures of their owners, much as a signet ring leaves a distinctive seal on hot wax.

All this took many days, and he was still only able to do tracking of the most rudimentary kind when the monsoon arrived.

As summer drew on dark clouds piled up beyond Kangchenjunga to the east, and on a day in mid-May they burst through the passes and came streaming west. In two hours they reached Mewa Khola, and amid lightning flashes and great rolls of thunder drenching rain swept over the farm-house, and the pastures, the peak of Topke, the cliffs, the forest ridge—everything around—disappeared in rain and mist.

'It's arrived!' cried Padamlal in relief to his wife. 'The monsoon has arrived!' He was soaked through as he splashed up from the terraced fields below, and fresh mud clung to his jodhpurs, but he was smiling broadly. 'There'll be more than enough rain this year—I can tell!' He looked with pleasure at the water spouting from the bamboo gutters, only this morning thick with the dust of dry-weather termites, and wiped his wet face and hair. 'Plenty of grazing after this,' he added with satisfaction, 'and the crops'll do well.' Neither he nor Ama mentioned the one terrible year before Aitahang was born, when the monsoon did not arrive. Then starvation had stared them in the face through that long summer of drought and the lean winter that followed. But this year the blue-black clouds gave promise of ample rain, and their spirits soared.

With the steady rain the yellow pastures grew green again and the flocks flourished, and all this time the little Tibetan mastiff puppy was growing as well. At first it just lolloped about the courtyard, occasionally clumsily stalking a hen as big as itself, and once facing up to a bad-tempered goat three times its size, when it had to be rescued by Ama. But gradually its soft woolly fur was changing to a harsh, stiff adult coat, the tough coat of a fighting dog, and by the end of summer, when the months of rain came to an end and weak gleams of watery sunshine shone on the sodden ridge above, Bhalu was half-grown, and already showing signs of the immense strength that would come in his second year. Soon his courage was to be convincingly demonstrated.

With the flock penned early one afternoon Aitahang had time to summon his friend Manbahadur from his farm less than a mile away, and the two boys discussed how best to spend the unexpected half-holiday. Aitahang had an idea. 'Let's see if we can get a partridge or two for supper! There are plenty of them up on the pasture.'

Manbahadur agreed with enthusiasm. 'The mist has gone completely—we'll take our pellet-bows!'

As the two boys prepared their little bows with their woven socket for launching small stones, Aitahang realized that Bhalu was wagging his tail and whining appealingly. 'Let's take him on *shikar*!' he said, and went to look for his father, and asked: 'Is it all right to take the dog up with us?'

'M'm, yes—I suppose so,' replied Padamlal. 'But don't let him run off on the scent of a musk-deer, or maybe something bigger!'

Aitahang promised, and with a run the three of them set off up the steep hill-side.

Alas for their hopes of sport! The high pasture was empty of partridge. 'We're too late in the day for them,' Aitahang admitted at last. 'They'll be up sheltering in the edge of the woods.' The two boys looked solemnly at the dark mass of trees several hundred feet higher up. They would not go in there without good reason, for in the trees lurked the big animals, and maybe other things as well, things like the Forest Man, at whose passing the birds and beasts fell silent. At least the forest did not hold the dreaded Sokpa, for he lived much higher, in the ice and snow.

The boys knew about the Sokpa now, having been told in whispers by their elder brothers. 'He is big,' they were told, 'bigger than a man. He lives in caves in the ice and'—final terrifying detail—'he is covered in red hair!'

Resignedly the boys prepared to return downhill again, but in a last glance round, Aitahang's eyes rested on the line of rock edging the top of the cliff at the end of the pasture. 'There's a black eagle's eyrie somewhere on that cliff face,' he said thoughtfully. 'I wonder . . . perhaps we might see it if we looked over.'

For a moment Manbahadur looked doubtful. He was thinking that partridges were one thing, but black eagles were quite another, then he nodded. 'Just a look over, then—nothing more!'

'Right. Come on, Bhalu!' The three of them hurried across the face of the pasture and slowed down as they threaded their way among the rocky outcrops of the clifftop. They knelt and cautiously peered over. 'Ahmai!' breathed Aitahang. 'You get a view from here!' The farm-house looked tiny below them, and in the sparkling air, washed clean of every speck of dust by the three months of rain, the snowy slopes of Topke stood out in crystal clarity, every ridge and crevasse clear and sharp. Across the Mewa the stretch of forest stood dark green, with here and there bamboo clumps gleaming a paler jade-like green among the trees. In the high silence the two boys could hear the roar of the glacier-fed Mewa, with through it a sharper hissing note. 'Sounds like a waterfall somewhere in those trees across the river,' commented Aitahang. 'Ever been across there?'

Manbahadur shook his head. 'No reason to go there, Aitey, none of our animals stray across the river. Besides, that wooded clump is the old Phedangba's land.'

'What does he use it for?' queried Aitahang. 'There's nothing there—no house or cultivation.'

'He gathers a bit of firewood, and sometimes does his *pujas* up there.' Manbahadur shrugged. That wild bit of land did not interest him much. 'Now, what about this eagle of yours?'

Flat on their stomachs they worked their way to the edge of the cliff and peered over, while Bhalu, leaning well back, edged up to them, his short ears pricked up, and growling at the empty space in front.

'Can't see a thing,' said Manbahadur.

Below them the rock face bulged outwards, hiding whatever lay beneath. Beyond the bulge the boys saw only glimpses of white water and rocks a thousand feet below.

'There's a bit of a ledge a bit farther along.' Aitahang nudged Manbahadur and pointed. 'Can you see it? If we get down on to it we'll be able to see what's below this overhang.'

Manbahadur looked where Aitahang pointed. He saw a narrow, uneven ledge a little way along the cliff face and a few feet below them.

'M'm.' He sounded very doubtful. 'I dare say we could, but—'

'But what?'

'If we miss the ledge we won't stop till we land on those rocks in the Mewa.'

'I want to see where that eagle went.' Aitahang spoke with

determination. 'Give me a hand down.' He moved along the cliff top a few feet and began letting himself slowly down backwards over the rock edge. Bhalu whined in anxiety, and Manbahadur held an arm tight.

'Tell me how far I've to go.'

'Not very far—about a couple of feet. But take it steady.'

'All right.' Aitahang twisted his head round and looked down for the ledge. For a moment he looked beyond it to the terrifying space below, and for the first time began to think himself foolhardy and rash. The ledge was not broad enough to stop him if he slipped. He pressed himself flat against the rough rock face and felt it grip him, scratching his chest as he slid slowly down. On down he went then suddenly felt the ledge with his bare feet and let it take his weight. He looked up, smiled at Manbahadur and at the comically concerned expression on Bhalu's face above him. Then he looked to his right and his smile vanished.

The overhang covered a recess, a shallow cave filled with what looked like a big bundle of brushwood, and in this coarse nest sat a pair of young birds, their downy heads and curved beaks jerking this way and that in curiosity. Above them, standing with wings half open and great beak forward, was a black eagle as big as himself.

Aitahang neither moved nor spoke. He knew that he was in mortal danger, and made no reply to Manbahadur's anxious call. With a rattle of pinions the eagle launched itself into space, soared away over the Mewa, banked, wheeled and dived straight at him. Aitahang clutched at the rock face with his hands while above him Manbahadur jumped and flailed his arms and Bhalu barked and snapped. Startled, the eagle swerved away, soaring up out again over the gorge of the Mewa.

'Watch out—it's coming back!' Frantically Manbahadur shouted and waved his arms, but this time the eagle knew what to expect and, brushing the cliff edge, dived straight at Aitahang from above. As the huge bird swept down at him Aitahang struck out at it with his bare hands, nearly overbalancing as he did so, and once again the eagle swerved away, but its talons slashed past Aitahang's head, just missing him. He flattened himself against the rock face again, despairingly preparing for the third attack—an attack he knew would topple him from the ledge. The eagle soared up and round, wheeled and swept down—but as Aitahang braced himself for the shock a shaggy demon shot up like a spring from the cliff edge, and with a perfection of timing a pair of powerful jaws snapped shut on a black wing. Dog and eagle, locked together, fell back on to the cliff edge. There was a squawking scream of surprise and rage, wings battered at the dog and talons tore at him, but he hung on. Manbahadur lashed at the eagle with his pellet-bow, Bhalu fell back with his mouth full of feathers, and the eagle broke loose, struggled to the cliff edge and launched itself once more into space—but this time to glide unevenly away out of sight.

'Quick, Aitey—grab the bow!' Manbahadur leant over and helped Aitahang to drag himself up the rock face and over the edge to safety and for some moments two very relieved boys lay panting and speechless.

'Bhalu,' said Aitahang, forcing himself to sit up and wiping the sweat of exertion from his face with his little white cap, 'you saved me, Bhalu—and so did you, my friend.'

'It was the dog,' said Manbahadur, 'and he's been hurt.'

'Quick, let's have a look at him.' Gently the two boys examined the young dog. 'No,' said Aitahang, 'he's all right.' Bhalu had a ruffled look about him, and mangled feathers hung about his jaws, but apart from a graze near his muzzle he was unhurt—his tough, thick coat had resisted the eagle's talons, and the battering wings had done him no damage whatsoever. He seemed quite unconcerned now, merely sniffing curiously at the feathers and poking his nose sideways over the cliff edge. Aitahang laughed: 'He can smell that nest of chicks!'

'Come on down,' said Manbahadur. 'Let them stay there!'

Laughing now, the boys stood up and brushed grass and feathers from each other. Then the three of them sprang off down the steep pastures for home.

'You've been a long time away,' observed Padamlal curiously. 'Find anything?'

'There wasn't a single partridge anywhere, Father,' answered Aitahang with perfect truth.

'Good-bye, then,' said Manbahadur with a half-wink. 'I must get back for supper,' and he trotted off with a wave of the hand.

'The weather's clear now,' Padamlal went on, 'you'll come with Balahang and me this time.'

'Where to, Father?' asked Aitahang in mounting excitement.

'To the autumn bazaar at Taplejung. We'll set off tomorrow!'

# 3 GODS AND HEROES

The whole family spent that evening gathering the crop of chillies from their bushes and packing them carefully between layers of broad leaves into cone-shaped baskets, called dokos, a big one for Padamlal to carry, and much smaller ones for the two boys. That night Aitahang could hardly sleep for excitement. But thoughts of the journey were interrupted by stark memories of those eight-foot black wings beating at his head, and the slashing strike of talons—till at last healthy fatigue won, and suddenly it was grey dawn and his brother was prodding him through the bearskin. 'Wake up! Anyone would think you didn't want to go!' and Aitahang sprang up, the eagle forgotten, his mind filled only with the thrill of his first journey from home.

After an early meal of curds and boiled maize, father and sons prepared to set off. Padamlal wore his own special kukri, then sharpened his big firewood kukri and hung it just inside the door. 'There, Mother—for any robber who comes round!' He nodded at Bhalu. 'That dog's growing up—and he looks as if he could use his teeth already!'

It was all Aitahang could do to stop himself shouting out that Bhalu had vanquished a black eagle, but with difficulty he kept quiet. Padamlal noticed nothing, however, and went on, 'Time to go—the sun's just up!'

The three dokos had been placed upright on a low bank, and father and sons stood each with his back against his own basket, and adjusted his namlo. This was the headstrap, a broad strap of fine-woven cane, flexible yet stronger than the strongest rope. One end went round the lower end of the basket, the other was slipped up over the shoulders and onto the forehead. While climbing this kept the doko pulled tight against the back, yet allowed the hands to remain free. By tightening or slackening the namlo subtle variations in the point of balance of the doko's weight could be made, resting some muscles while changing to others.

'Ready, Sons?' asked Padamlal.

'Ready, Father,' replied the two boys.

'Hup!' And they leant forward into their namlos and took the weight against their backs.

'Be careful on the way!' urged Ama anxiously. She thought of rushing torrents, thieves and robbers, cheats in the bazaar, avalanches on the track—all sorts of very real dangers.

'We'll be careful,' grunted Padamlal impatiently. 'Let's go!'

It was the first time in his life that Aitahang had been out of his home valley. They struck across the hill-side to meet the crest of the downward-sloping ridge, then followed it down steeply—hard work this, he found, straining back against the slope with a load on his back—down and down to where the Mewa drove violently into the course of a river flowing fast and greeny white from the north-east. 'This is the Sona,' shouted Padamlal, mopping his face as they sat to rest before crossing. Even as he rested, Aitahang felt his legs twitch and tremble at the unaccustomed strain. Yet his basket was only a fraction of the weight of his father's—packed solid with produce and so heavy that to lift it his father had to seat himself on the ground with the basket against the slope, then struggle upright while the great muscles in his thighs and calves bulged into hard pads. Down here where the rivers met was rather like sitting in a deep, very noisy cavern. The racing water surged green and the spray sprang white against the rocks, all with a steady roaring against which they had to shout to be heard.

'How can we cross?'

'There's a cantilever bridge about half a mile farther up.' They set off for it, passing clumps of trees and a big grove of bamboo growing wild above the water. The bridge was a fearsome-looking affair, axe-trimmed logs stacked up outwards from both banks, each log projecting a little farther than the last till one final log was lashed across the remaining central gap. A long cane handrail hung swaying in a slack loop roughly along the line of bridge. The logs were dark wet, and slippery with spray. 'I'll go first,' called Padamlal above the noise, and set off up the edifice, step by steady step. He reached the far side safely, then turned to watch anxiously as Aitahang began the journey across. Twice the boy felt his bare feet slip, each time he recovered, but he was trembling with strain when he finally stepped down on to solid ground again. Balahang crossed safely and they all set off at once up the long climb to the crest high above, relieved to be away from that dangerous river. At the top they paused a moment and Aitahang turned to glance back over the winding Mewa.

Burdened as he was he could not resist stopping to stare. Till now he had vaguely accepted that the 'Himal' that grown-ups referred to meant the white crest of Topke at the end of his own valley of the Mewa. Now, suddenly and overwhelmingly, he saw from this high vantage point the real Himal. Nothing had prepared the impressionable little boy for the sweeping infinity of snow pierced by numberless glittering ice-peaks, the lower slopes striped dark where rock showed through, black cliffs too steep for snow to lie. Somewhere at the foot of this his once-impressive pinnacle of Topke stood modestly, no more than a foothill, its ridges running back and disappearing into giant ice-walls.

'Come on, Aitahang,' his father called impatiently, stooping under his load. 'It's too cold to hang about—and we'll never arrive at this rate.' To Padamlal the Himal was unknown country, freezing cold and quite impossible for men (though not for Sokpas or for holy men from Tibet). The Himal provided no food, no grazing for cattle, only blizzards in winter and always the icy breath of glaciers. But to Aitahang the sudden vision was a revelation, a glimpse of a magic country, unattainable, beautiful and deadly. Now he knew where the Gods lived. Krishna, the Hindu Shepherd-God, might flirt with milkmaids by ferny waterfalls, but that high and frozen wilderness enthroned a starker deity, his handmaidens the blizzards and the clouds.

The rest of that day's journey passed for him in a haze of growing fatigue, and when they at last unburdened themselves of their dokos in the village duty-house at Lingten Aitahang flopped down, leant his head against his basket and fell asleep at once, his sweaty shirt cooling chill on him. His father covered him with a small strip of woollen blanket, shaking his head in compassion. He remembered his own childhood: he too had carried a doko to Taplejung from the same valley as a little boy and he too had been too exhausted to stay awake, even to eat a handful of maize. Life was hard in the Gurkha hills, even for children. But there was no other way; unless everyone worked from sun-up till nightfall they would go hungry—and carrying the doko was the heaviest task of all.

The next morning they were up and away from Lingten by daybreak and by full light were padding along a good path above the foaming Mewa. At first Aitahang was stiff and weary from yesterday, but the first mile of hard slog under the heavy basket warmed him, seeming to oil his muscles. The path, being level enough, was easier yet he longed for another huge hill to climb for another glimpse of the Himal. Before midday they were across the wide Tambur—by a better bridge this time, a suspension bridge with a proper handrail of cable—and toiling up the north face of the Taplejung slope. When they were high up Aitahang turned a moment to gaze, but his hopes of another vision of the snows were dashed: today storm-clouds were raging high above the wooded ridges, and peaks and glaciers were hidden. This made his vision of yesterday all the more precious; he realized that the snows were not always in easy view—his deity was changeable, aloof and moody. But the packed, cobbled streets of Taplejung were close above them now, and his mind turned with excitement to this new experience.

Taplejung bazaar was quite unlike anything Aitahang had expected. What surprised him most were the shopkeepers—they looked so foreign. Instead of the taut, wheat-coloured, high-cheekboned faces and narrow slanting eyes of the Limbus they were darker-skinned, with softer, rounder features and larger eyes which curved like those of oxen. Also, they were sleek and plump and their skins had an oily sheen, again quite unlike the lean-flanked Limbus with their bulging thigh and calf muscles.

'These bazaar people are Newars,' muttered Padamlal in a low voice to the boys. 'They originally came from the valley around Katmandu. They have the money, these shopkeepers, they have the money. But,' he added in some satisfaction, 'they're not like us when it comes to courage.'

Leaving his load with the boys Padamlal roamed the streets, bargaining with shopkeepers for the loads of chillies and at length returned, not too dissatisfied. 'Fair price from one of them,' he grunted, and hoisting up their loads they made for the shop which was to take their produce.

It was a spice shop, and it smelt wonderful. There were big, open-mouthed baskets of chillies, red and green, fresh and dried; smaller, shallow baskets held coriander, nutmeg, cardamom—all sorts of exotic rich-smelling seeds and leaves, as well as cinnamon bark, peppercorns and, to Aitahang most delectable of all, bundles of ginger root. His father was paid in Indian rupee notes and the shopkeeper produced for the boys small squares of sticky sweets; when he saw Aitahang stowing one away in his cummerbund to take home for his sister he made up a special package for her.

Their selling done, Padamlal took the boys with him as he bought supplies to carry back, kerosene, cloth and salt, then, these purchases made, they stacked their loads and wandered about the bazaar.

Here and there as they sauntered past the shops Aitahang heard the comforting accents of his own mother-tongue, but others with the same features as themselves spoke in the language he recognized as the mountain language, Gurkhali. Though quite different from the Limbu language it was beginning to sound familiar to him with repeated hearing, and he found himself understanding snatches of it here and there. 'Who are these?' he whispered to his father, nodding surreptitiously to a group talking Gurkhali. 'They're not Limbus—but they're not Newars, either.'

'They look like Tamangs,' replied his father. 'They live all across the hills. They're Buddhists, like the Tibetans, and'—he grinned—'they're *nearly* as good as us!' He jerked his chin across to another group. 'Now they're Rais. They're like us, and we can inter-marry with them. They come from west of the Tambur

Khola, most of them. You must be careful with them, for Rais are very hot-tempered. They don't fight any better than Limbus—just quicker!'

Balahang smiled at all this. He was quite an experienced traveller now, and had been to Taplejung three times, and was quite used to the different tribes and clans of the area. Aitahang, however, was still wide-eyed at the press of people, most of them country folk like themselves, with an occasional Brahmin priest with caste mark on cheek and forehead. One group, however, he could not place.

There were five of them, all young men and all Limbus, but there was something about them that caught his attention, and he did not know what this was. It wasn't so much their clothing, though they were well—to him richly—dressed, with clean new hill clothing, jackets of good dark cloth, long woollen scarves of varied colours, hill caps and Limbu kukris. Watching them surreptitiously he realized that they did not gape about them like the country boys who had carried in their dokos to market, but had an air of quiet confidence, talking easily with the shopkeepers and with passing acquaintances. Also they seemed bigger than the other Limbus, heavier and sunburnt. He touched his father's arm: 'Who are those men?' he whispered. 'Where do they come from?'

Padamlal looked across to where Aitahang indicated with a shift of his chin, and said to him quietly, 'They'll be soldiers on leave. We'll see more now that the monsoon is over and the travelling season has begun again.' He looked down at Aitahang, noting the wide eyes and the fascinated stare. 'Don't envy them too much, my son, a soldier's life is hard and dangerous.'

'Have they come from a war, Father?'

'The last big war is over, but it is said that there are many small wars in its place. And remember,' he warned, 'in the end the soldier only finds wounds and death.'

Aitahang barely heard him. His mind was far away and his imagination busy, till Padamlal interrupted him, saying, 'We've something else to get.'

'What is it, Father?'

'You'll see.'

Aitahang looked at Balahang, but he only smiled and shook his head. It was all very mysterious, and the young boy followed his father and brother in great curiosity as they threaded their way through the press till they neared the end of the shops. Here they came to clusters of open booths selling cigarettes and matches and betel-nut and trinkets and garish pictures of Hindu deities. Standing among these booths were two or three men in hill dress but with darker skins and narrow, Indian-looking features, holding slim bundles wrapped in cloth. Padamlal stopped before one of these and said to Aitahang with the faintest twinkle in his eye, 'These men are Kamis—artificers in metal.'

Aitahang said nothing. He was refusing to let himself jump to conclusions. He watched and listened as Padamlal said to one of the Kamis, 'Let's see 'em—I'm looking for something not too big.' The Kami unwrapped his bundle and Aitahang felt his heart go thud, but still he kept his face expressionless. After all, he was a Limbu of eight years, and no longer a child to show excitement.

But in spite of himself his eyes glistened, for from the cloth emerged three kukris, newly forged, their long blades gleaming from the polishing stone except for the broad cutting edge, ground grey to razor sharpness.

'H'm,' grunted Padamlal, 'not too bad.' He examined the scabbards. 'Yes, leather quite good . . .' He hefted a kukri in his hand and said thoughtfully, 'I really wanted something a little smaller.' The one he held in his hand had a curving blade of about twelve inches in length, and the Kami looked surprised: anything much shorter would lack the necessary weight when swung.

Padamlal looked at the kukri again. It was a good one, the blade only slightly curved forward, the handle shaped in the Limbu style, with a more slender grip than the kukris of other tribes, yet ending in a broad butt. Also, the handle was of beautifully polished wood, the grain clearly marked. Although bigger than he had wanted for Aitahang, it tempted him; after all, the boy would eventually be big enough to handle it easily. 'How much?' he asked.

For a moment the Kami did not answer. He looked at the Limbu farmer and his sons, at the gaunt, weather-beaten faces, the patched clothing and the bare feet, and sighed to himself. Bargaining was no use—fancy prices would just send them away. He must state the correct price, the price which would not be too much for them, yet which would repay him for his work as well as the cost of the steel, the wood for the handle, the charcoal for his fire and the leather scabbard made to fit by the leather-worker (for he as a metal worker could not work in leather, nor had he the skill to do so). 'Huzoor,' he replied, 'the price is six rupees.'

Padamlal shook his head and handed the kukri back, saying, 'Too much—six rupees is a terrible price for a kukri,' and behind him Aitahang felt his heart sink. Six rupees was a vast sum; he had no right to expect the family to spend so much on him. He stared down at the ground, but looked up quickly again as he heard his father say to another of the Kamis, 'Let's see what you've got.'

His kukris were also good ones, and one in particular made Padamlal forget himself so far as to mutter aloud, 'What a beauty!' It was delicate and slender, and clearly would never be used to chop wood. This was a real warrior's kukri—but it was out of the question for Aitahang, as the blade compensated for its slenderness by being some fourteen inches long. Padamlal held it and turned it over and flexed his wrist and murmured in admiration: it balanced like a feather, yet swung down like an axe. He shook his head sadly: what a pity it was not for work as well.

The Kami said to him in a significant tone, 'And, Huzoor—the handle is of buffalo-horn.' Padamlal looked at the bluish-grey handle and nodded. He knew what the Kami meant: buffalo-horn handles were much prized by Gurkha fighting men, as they did not become slippery when blood-stained. He handed it back with a sigh. A weapon like that might cost anything up to twelve or fourteen rupees. Some of these young men on leave from soldiering might afford it, but not he. Anyway, he realized with relief, it was not only too big for Aitahang but was wrong for him. A shepherd-boy needed to cut bamboo, to slash grass, to cut himself branches for a shelter in bad weather, to whittle wood, and to protect himself from marauding animals. He wouldn't be killing men with it—though a Gurkha must always be ready to defend himself to the death. He turned, his mind made up.

'Here,' he grunted to the first Kami, 'let's see that first one again.'

Aitahang watched, his muscles taut with the tension of it all. Without a word his father turned round, gripped the boy's cummerbund and tucked through it the kukri in its scabbard, then paid the Kami six single rupee notes. The Kami touched his forehead with the money in salutation, Padamlal jerked his head and father and sons walked back to the main bazaar.

It was past midday. The business of the market was at its height and the numbers great. The drink shops had been busy, and Aitahang saw with distaste one or two drunks swaying and staggering on the fringes of the crowds, their faces pink with the effects of the powerful rice spirit sold for a rupee in bottles containing just under a pint. 'They've wasted their money,' said Padamlal in scorn. 'Come on—we'll pick up our loads and get off home.' The two boys stuck to him closely as he pushed through the crowds, then stopped with him as he paused where a thicker knot of spectators were grouped round something or somebody. 'What's this?' Inside the group someone was speaking in a loud voice. Aitahang stood on tiptoe but could see nothing except men's backs, so he bent down and peered between their legs. He couldn't see very well, but he made out a grey-haired man with a Limbu kukri in his cummerbund seated cross-legged on a mat and looking up at the attentive faces round him. He was declaiming in the Limbu language and Aitahang picked up snatches of what he was saying '... the true story of the great prince, Jangbahadur . . . Listen, please listen . . .' He held out a metal bowl, repeating, 'Hear the story of Rajah Jangbahadur! Hear how he slew the elephant, how he slaughtered his enemies, how he became the thrice-worthy ruler of all Nepal . . .' He passed round his bowl and two or three men put small copper coins in it. He glanced at them and called out, 'Silver, my masters—will some gentleman give silver for the story of Jangbahadur? Here, sir—' and he proffered the bowl to a big Limbu standing in the forefront—'Big man, big heart!' The Limbu grinned sheepishly and put a silver four-anna piece in the bowl. The old story-teller cried, 'My respects! And now I begin!'

Padamlal pulled his two sons round in front of him and, squashed though they were between the men, they were able surreptitiously to squeeze to the front where they squatted down, mouths open and eyes fixed on the story-teller's face. Neither Padamlal nor the boys considered for a moment beginning their journey back without hearing this. Of Jangbahadur Padamlal had heard occasionally, mainly in snatches of song at festival time. The two boys had never heard of him at all.

Once satisfied that his audience were attentive the story-teller began his tale. He opened with preliminary flourishes describing Jangbahadur's ancestry and how he—the son of a minor nobleman at the court in Katmandu—became an officer in the Royal Army. He was young and bold, said the story-teller, and went on, 'Soon the senior officers became jealous of his great prowess, and accused him of plotting against the King himself, so he was sent away from the capital in disgrace, exiled to the Terai, where they hoped he might die of fever, or be killed by the arrows of the wild Tharus, or be eaten by a man-eater.'

The listening men said not a word. All knew of the low-lying stretch of forest called the Terai where the Nepal Himalayas swept down to the plains of Hindustan—a forest where malaria killed men, where Tharu aborigines lived with bows and arrows, and where each year the Nepalese court held great hunts for the enormous tigers that abounded there—hunts from elephant-back.

'So Jangbahadur was exiled to the Western Terai. But he did not die of fever, nor was he killed by arrows, nor was he eaten by tigers. Instead, the Terai people called on him to deliver them from an elephant that had gone mad and was ravaging their crops. Jangbahadur therefore took his musket and loaded it with a single ball, and went to find the elephant, alone and on foot.'

Aitahang sat still as a stone. He was far away down in the Terai, approaching a mad elephant on foot, armed with only a musket.

'The elephant heard Jangbahadur and ran towards him, to spear him with his tusks and then to throw him in the air and at last to stamp on him, as he had stamped on so many poor farmers. But Jangbahadur had heard the secret of killing elephants.' The story-teller looked round the circle of absorbed faces. 'He knew that there is one place, and only one, where one must hit a charging elephant.' He paused and the listening men leant forward expectantly. 'That place,' went on the story-teller in a low, confidential tone, 'is small, no bigger than the little dish which holds your spices at a feast. It is in the middle of the forehead where the bone is thin, above and between the eyes—' Aitahang quickly put his hand up and touched the same spot on his own forehead—'and Jangbahadur took careful aim.' He paused, and the listening crowd held their breath. 'He aimed, masters, and he fired. His aim was true, and his musket ball struck the very spot and pierced through to the brain. Like a mountain the elephant fell dead!'

As one man the listeners hissed out their relief. Aitahang gulped; he had been too excited to breathe.

'Once his prowess had been shown,' went on the story-teller, 'the Terai people begged Jangbahadur rid them of other menaces

—man-eating tigers, and even the Terai bandits who live on extortion and robbery. One by one Jangbahadur faced them, and in a series of desperate fights killed them all off. Finally, to prevent him becoming too popular, and perhaps gathering a following of his own, the King reluctantly summoned him back to Katmandu.'

Aitahang listened entranced; this was real adventure—beside it the homely tasks of shepherding seemed very tame.

'So Jangbahadur returned to the capital, my masters, still poor, still without a following of men—but with honour, and with fame. Many young men of the hills who had only kukri or *konra* to make their fortune swore that they would follow when he called.' The story-teller paused and took a long swig of raksi from the bamboo container beside him. 'The throat gets dry,' he commented, then eyeing the increased numbers pressing around to hear his tale he shrewdly held out his bowl. Seeing that he would not continue until he had received further contributions the listeners reluctantly fumbled for small coins, and eventually the story-teller continued.

'He was a Captain, no more and no less—but a man without fear. Knowing this the King, although he hated him, had Jangbahadur kill certain of his enemies, saying, "Obey or die yourself". A hard choice, my masters—but what was he to do? So he killed at the King's bidding.'

The old man described in lengthy detail the bold and bloody adventures by which Jangbahadur progressed in the King's service while all the time building up his own following, eventually making himself a general in command of several regiments of Gurkha troops.

'But all this time,' went on the old story-teller, 'Jangbahadur knew of the King's enmity, and at length his opportunity came. A dispute had arisen between the King and his Queen over a favourite of hers, the Chief Minister. Because the King hated the Queen he had this man killed—we do not know by whom. But the Queen gathered the nobles, and the leaders of the Kingdom, to turn them against the King. They all met in the courtyard of the palace, that called the Hanuman Dhoka, because of the carving of the God Hanuman beside the strong wooden door. The Queen demanded that the one responsible for the killing be punished, and accusations and counter-accusations were made, and fighting broke out. But, my masters, one man had prepared for trouble.' The story-teller looked round. The crowd about him was still as stone.

'Jangbahadur had prudently kept his regiments ready not far away. When the first blade was drawn he sprang up on to the Queen's balcony, and signalled for his men. Below him in the courtyard the fighting became general, every man against his neighbour. No one knew who was friend and who was enemy, and even brothers cut at each other in the fury of the fight! Ah, my masters, the slaughter was terrible! The nobles and high officers were armed each with his own personal kukri or konra, or even with sharp swords captured from the English in the earlier wars—and all were fierce fighters. From outside passers-by tried to open the door but it was bolted—and from beneath the door blood ran out into the street.' He paused and took a long swig of raksi.

'Then Jangbahadur's regiments arrived,' he went on. 'They quickly broke in the door and seized the few survivors. Jangbahadur had defended himself on the balcony, and lived. He was now the strong one, my masters—and it was not long before he expelled both King and Queen from the country, to Benares, where they lived and plotted uselessly, while Jangbahadur ruled Nepal, living for forty years more and even going to England to see the Great Queen of that country.'

The story-teller paused and once again drank. 'A stirring tale, my masters, of the great prince Jangbahadur Rana! Is is not worth silver? Be generous, my masters—' With a mixture of flattery and calls for their generosity he held out his bowl once more but the audience, seeing that this time the story of Jangbahadur was really over, drifted away. With a sigh the old man put down his bowl again and shifted on his mat. With a start of horror Aitahang saw that he only had one leg. The story-teller looked up and caught Aitahang's gaze, looked at his stump of leg and nodded sadly. 'Yes, I have only one leg, son; the other I lost in a big war, far away.' He sighed and took another long drink of raksi. 'Yes,' he said, 'far away, fighting for the Angrezi, the British Sahibs, many years ago—so many I have forgotten.'

Aitahang asked in reluctant fascination, 'Where was this war?'

'It was in a far-away country called Frantsi, in cold and mud. But where do you come from, boy?'

'From Mewa Khola.'

'Where along Mewa Khola—Changa? Lingten?'

'Phangma.'

'Ah—right up towards Topke.' The old man gave Aitahang a

sideways glance. 'That's up where the Sokpa lives, and the Forest Man. Do you know about the Sokpa, boy?'

Aitahang stayed silent, shifting from one leg to the other. This talk about the Sokpa made him uneasy and, besides, the story-teller was beginning to look rather drunk. He started to move away to where his father and brother were chatting to two other Limbus, hearing the latest news of the destructive Kabeli leopard, but the old man called after him, 'Do you hear the Sokpa whistle, boy—in the dead of night?' He wheezed sadly to himself. 'When I was young I used to climb high to the snow-line, but I never saw one . . .' He mumbled on to himself and took another long swig of raksi, and Aitahang seized the chance to escape to his father.

'Time to go.' Padamlal bade farewell to his friends and led the two boys to where their dokos were stacked in safety by the trader's shop. 'Just check,' he reminded the boys. 'See that the namlo is correctly adjusted and isn't frayed at all—for a break as one is walking along a cliff-edge path or crossing one of these bridges would be a disaster.' He checked his own namlo as he spoke, and the boys did the same. 'Next see to your loads,' he went on. 'Make sure that nothing is going to protrude against your back, and rub or chafe. It's bad enough carrying the load without it being painful as well.' He himself looked over the boys' loads and satisfied himself that they were correctly settled into the cone-shaped baskets. Balahang had one full tin of kerosene, just as much as he could manage, and Aitahang carried the bundle of salt and the wrapped-up cloth for the ladies of the farm, a bulkier but much lighter load. 'Right,' said Padamlal, and they settled themselves, with backs against their dokos, and slipped the namlos up round their foreheads. 'Hup!' Forward they leant into their loads, took the strain, then muscles taut, slowly stood erect. 'Home!' said Padamlal.

On the long haul down to Lingten, Aitahang was only partially conscious of the heavy doko on his back. His mind was full of the kukri thrust diagonally through the front of his cummerbund. It seemed huge to him, the brass-tipped end of the leather scabbard sticking out beyond his right hip and the handle resting half against his chest, but he would grow, he kept telling himself—he would grow. As it was he could use the kukri even now, and surreptitiously took his right hand from the namlo and gripped the kukri handle. Even at this slight touch the kukri seemed to vibrate, as if ready to jump out at the slightest pull. At Lingten that evening, weary from the long, exciting day so full of new sights and experiences, he held himself from sleep long enough to draw the blade and feast his eyes on it. Cautiously he swung it, and he realized with delight that even though yet far too big for him, it balanced perfectly, and the slender Limbu handle almost seemed made for his small hand. With a curving push he thrust it back into the scabbard again, and as soon as he had swallowed his supper of maize and a handful of green beans he rolled himself in his blanket and fell asleep. When Padamlal quietly looked to see that he was sleeping soundly, he saw the new kukri clutched in Aitahang's arms.

Up and away early from Lingten the next morning they toiled up towards the ridge, on the way meeting a dozen or so lads hurrying along in single file, with an older man at their head. Aitahang and his brother stared, for they were travelling fast and carrying no loads. 'What are they doing, Father?' asked Aitahang when they were past. 'They're not carrying anything?'

Padamlal spoke disapprovingly. 'That's a *Galla*, my son—a party of young lads going off to enlist in the army. After harvest is the time they go, after the harvest every year.'

Aitahang would have liked to question his father further on this: where were they heading, why did they hurry so, who was the older man, but they breasted the ridge and he forgot as the panorama of Himal opened out before them.

Again Aitahang caught his breath at their vastness, in particular at one peak that seemed to stand back, as if remote; a peak so high that the snow did not lie on it, but streamed out like a torn white prayer flag from its dark rock flanks. His father and brother also paused a moment, and Aitahang asked, 'Father, do these peaks have names?'

'Some do have names,' answered Padamlal, 'but only these Sherpas know them—for they were named by the holy lamas of Tibet. I do not know them, though one, it is said, is called Mother Goddess of the World, of the Country where No Birds Fly.' He sighed from beneath his doko. 'We have little time for such mysteries.' He gripped his namlo and padded off.

All morning they followed the tiny winding path, and by early afternoon they were descending the last steep section before the cantilever bridge. 'You cross first, this time, Aitahang,' ordered his father, 'and I will watch from this side.' He propped his staff behind him to take the weight of his doko and watched from under his namlo as the young boy carefully began the slippery crossing. This time Aitahang felt more confidence; his load was a trifle lighter and although the logs were as slippery with spray as ever he trod them steadily and reached the far side without mishap, then turned to watch his brother.

Balahang was nearly two-thirds across when it happened. Whether his load shifted or his foot slipped a trifle, or both, Aitahang could not see. All he saw was his brother tumble from the end of the highest log and fall, doko and all, into the foaming water below.

On the far bank Padamlal threw off his doko and plunged straight into the torrent, but it swept him from his feet and dashed him against a rock, half-stunning him, so that he was able to do no more than cling to it and struggle weakly to keep from being dragged down. Balahang was still conscious; the shock of his fall had been taken by his doko, which hit the water first, but he was being battered by the water and was being dragged scrabbling against the rock shelves a foot or two below the surface. In a few moments he would be too weak to keep his partial hold, and would be plucked away and swept to his death.

Aitahang threw off his doko and started to run blindly down into the torrent—then checked himself as he reached the rock edge. He would achieve nothing that way. He scrambled back, looking desperately right and left for help. He shouted, in case someone heard him, but his cries were drowned in the hissing roar of the torrent. Below him Padamlal was painfully pulling himself through the white water towards Balahang, some ten yards from him, but Aitahang could see only too clearly that his brother was weakening. In a few moments he would lose his precarious hold on the underwater rock face, and would be swept away towards the junction of the Mewa and the Sona, where nothing could survive. Aitahang felt powerless to help; in a moment his brother would be drowned before his eyes—then as if from a great distance a voice boomed though his head '. . . a bamboo grove offers deliverance'. He turned and raced along the twisty path above the river, to the clump of growing bamboos he had passed on the outward journey, some eighty yards below the bridge.

He had never run so fast in his life. He reached the bamboos, instinctively chose a young, pale green bamboo for its lightness, plucked out his new kukri, and with two slashing cuts severed the bamboo and raced back again. Even as he ran he saw his brother's head vanish below the water, bob up again yards downstream, then vanish again. Aitahang sprang to the edge and thrust the bamboo across, wedging it against a rock. The current plucked at it but he bore down with all his weight and in barely a moment he felt a thump against it. His brother was swung against the bamboo, threw a weak arm over it and managed to hold on, though his legs and body were swept trailing downstream. Then, ever so slowly, fighting for breath against the water which foamed round and over him, he pulled himself along the bamboo till he reached the rock edge, and Aitahang grabbed his cotton shirt and clung till Balahang dragged himself over and flopped exhausted on the rocks.

Aitahang then ran with the bamboo to where his father was slowly heaving himself up over the boulders in mid-stream and pushed it out towards him. Padamlal took it and, pulling himself along hand over hand, reached the rocky bank and hurried down to where his elder son lay coughing up water, pale and cold, but alive.

# 4 THE LEOPARD

Although Aitahang did not realize it, the river rescue marked for him not only the physical end of summer and the beginning of the cold, clear Himalayan autumn, but the end of his transition from childhood to responsible youth. His father gave him an increased share in the work of the farm and, as a young Gurkha armed with his own kukri, he had greater freedom to go off with his friend Manbahadur when his work was done. Together the boys hunted small animals with trap and bow, netted fish in the quieter pools of the Mewa, gazed with awe at the occasional soldier walking home on leave over the mountains, and once even made a daring but fruitless trip up into the high woods to look for the Forest Man.

Most of the time, however, it was work—grazing the flock, ploughing and sowing in due season, harvesting crops and carrying heavier and heavier dokos each year to the autumn bazaar at Taplejung. One thing that Aitahang continued, so that it became second nature with him, was his practice at tracking. Everywhere he went he occupied himself by studying the ground and the vegetation and drawing conclusions from what he saw. His eyes became trained to observe the minutest evidence, and he extended his observations beyond the tracks left by sheep and goats to the tracks of other animals, and even of men. He no longer had any difficulty in following animals that had strayed: he merely cast round till he found a print that he recognized, then followed it effortlessly till he came up to where the animal was lying out of sight.

So the years passed, busy always, but uneventful, till Aitahang reached his thirteenth birthday, not long after returning from an autumn journey to Taplejung. Manbahadur had also been there, and now they sat talking of what they had seen and, as they did more and more often now, speaking wistfully of travel and adventure in strange lands.

'There's a soldier on leave in Changa,' said Manbahadur idly, plucking a tall grass and tickling Bhalu's nose with it. 'He told me of a new war.'

'Oh, yes? Whereabouts?' Aitahang lay on his back, staring up at the cold blue sky. He felt restless and rather unsettled; no longer completely absorbed in his pastoral life. Although thirteen he was still only a boy, and very much second to Balahang, who would be getting married shortly, and who was already taking over more and more responsibility for the running of things. Balahang was a kind brother, but there was no disguising who was going to become master of the farm as their father grew older. 'Where is this war?' asked Aitahang, trying to turn his thoughts to something different.

'It is in Ma-la-ya,' said Manbahadur, pronouncing the unfamiliar name slowly.

'Who are fighting?'

'The Angrezi are fighting the Chini, and Gurkha sons are fighting for the Angrezi, as always.'

'What is it like?' asked Aitahang casually, but without much interest. He thought briefly back to the old story-teller, who had lost his leg fighting for the Angrezi. Their wars didn't seem to do Gurkhas much good—then again, though, there were those big strapping well-dressed men he saw occasionally; *they* looked well enough. And they got paid . . .

'The soldier says it is all forest fighting, men hunting men. He says it is very like *shikar*—but the quarry is armed, and very often waits in ambush.'

'Forest fighting?' Aitahang pondered a moment, then rolled over to watch Manbahadur and Bhalu having a lazy tug of war with twists of long grass. 'Like *shikar*, eh?' Although he spoke to Manbahadur he was really repeating this to himself, and thinking of another Gurkha who had won fame and eventually a kingdom from early bravery in the forests of the Terai. It was, of course, quite out of the question for him to think of going when he was old enough—the war would be over by then, and there was quite enough to do at home—but it did no harm to dream a little. But his thoughts were interrupted by the distant boom of the huge *chhebrung* drums, the Limbu invitation to all who heard to come and join a family's celebrations, whether a wedding, a christening or some other joyous function, and the two boys raced off with Bhalu, to take part and receive their share of the good things. Later, though, Aitahang found his thoughts returning more than once to the forest war in the unknown country called Ma-la-ya.

Then something happened which abruptly banished all such vague fancies from his mind. On a cold night in early winter the farm was raided by a leopard.

It was just before midnight when Bhalu's hysterical barking and furious springs against his chain, frightened baas from the sheep and a rush of hoofs in the pen jerked them from sleep. The two brothers scrambled down in a scatter of hay, Aitahang still with his fur cloaked about him and grasping his scabbarded kukri. Outside, the night was bright with moonlight and noisy with volleys of barks. At the far edge of the courtyard a lithe shadow sprang through a pool of moonlight and vanished in the overgrown thickets beyond.

'A light—bring a light!'

Aitahang dashed into the house, blew on the ash-covered embers of the fire, thrust in a resinous pine-knot and ran back again, holding the sputtering yellow flame above his head.

'Over here!' commanded his father's voice, and Aitahang hurried across to the pen.

'Did he take any?'

It was difficult to count the terrified animals, scrambling about in the blackness of the pen with the blazing pine-knot throwing shifting shadows everywhere, but at last they managed to quieten and count them.

'One gone,' said Padamlal grimly, 'and that's all he came for tonight.'

Aitahang ran across to the far edge of the courtyard and, holding the torch high peered out into the dark, but nothing moved and he returned to where the others stood in grim silence, unmindful of the freezing cold. One goat seemed no great loss, but they knew that this was only the first. At length Padamlal ordered: 'Get some sleep—that leopard won't be back tonight.'

Bhalu was quiet again, a sure sign that the leopard was far away. 'Good dog,' said Padamlal, patting him, 'you did well.' Then he climbed heavily up to reassure a worried Ama that all was more or less well, and that only one animal had been taken. But lying wrapped in his heavy plaid Padamlal slept only fitfully, his mind busy with worry. That must be the Kabeli leopard, the expert and murderous thief, probably driven away from his old hunting grounds and seeking new ones up here. He lay with open eyes, staring up into the darkness. So far no one had been able to stalk it, or even get a good shot at it; how could he, with his old muzzle-loader, hope to succeed where so many had failed? That leopard now knew where the flock was penned. It would ruin him, and perhaps maul or kill his children as well.

Dawn found him sleepless and weary, but determined, and he went down and said quietly to Balahang, 'Today we will hunt the leopard while the spoor is still fresh. That leopard dies—or we starve next year.'

In the growing light he went out beyond the sheep-pen and cast round in the direction the leopard had vanished. In a few minutes he returned with a grunt of satisfaction. 'Found a set of pug-marks where he jumped the fence carrying the goat—splayed-out, scarred pads. Looks like a big, old beast. He'll be cunning, too—must be that villain from across the Kabeli.' He went into the farm-house, took down his old muzzle-loader, rammed in powder, wadding and ball, set the cap and checked the priming, and stowed away spare powder and shot in his haversack. Then he took out his kukri, tested the edge, replaced it in his scabbard and thrust it diagonally through the front of his cummerbund.

'What are you going to do?' asked his wife with a look of alarm. 'You're not going after him?'

'We must get him, Wife, and we must get him quickly, or he'll do us terrible damage. And if we don't—' He just shook his head, and Aitahang saw his mother blink and nod. They had only themselves to rely on; no one else would save them from the leopard.

'I'll take Balahang,' said Palamlal. 'He can come behind me and keep a sharp lookout. Get ready, Son,' he said to the elder boy, 'we'll go at once.'

'Can I come too?' Aitahang tucked his kukri firmly into his cummerbund. 'I'll bring Bhalu—he'll help!'

Padamlal paused in his preparations and put a hand on Aitahang's shoulder. 'You must stay here, Son,' he said gently. 'Two of us are enough. And besides, Bhalu is a guard-dog, not a tracker dog. He might lead us off after a musk-deer, or a bear. I must track this leopard myself, and you and Bhalu will guard the farm and see to the grazing while we are away. There'll be plenty to do!'

Bitterly disappointed, Aitahang nevertheless nodded obediently, and after giving Bhalu a reassuring pat—at which the big dog whined in understanding—he joined his mother and sister in a silent group to watch while his father and brother climbed up beyond the farm-house in single file, eyes on the ground, till they disappeared over the crest leading to the high pasture.

'He'll be lying up in the high woods—they will soon kill him and bring back his skin,' said Aitahang comfortingly, but his mother turned away, her face drawn and worried. Not only was her husband out on the trail of this killer with an ancient gun that was half-useless, but her first-born was with him. 'Graze the animals close in today,' she called harshly to Aitahang. 'That devil may come back!'

All day long they waited in anxiety and hope for the sound of the shot that would signal the meeting with the leopard, but the hours passed in silence except for the faint cry of the buzzards and the distant wing-beats of the black eagle. The long silence began to get on their nerves: had the two men been attacked and mauled before they fired a shot? Their anxiety mounted as the hours of daylight passed, till at last, when the sharp afternoon light was weakening into dusk, there was a welcoming bark from Bhalu, and they saw two figures coming slowly down the low pasture. Aitahang ran to meet them, but his eager question remained unasked: their blank faces showed that they had failed.

'We lost the tracks,' said Padamlal down at the farm-house, as he was unloading his gun. 'We followed them right up to the edge of the high woods, by the big fallen pine, where we found the remains of the goat. Then we lost them.' He sat down wearily. 'We'll try again tomorrow.'

'Don't you go out after him any more!' cried Ama. 'We'll put Bhalu beside the pen at night—he'll warn us!' But she spoke without conviction, and Padamlal answered soberly, 'The leopard would just wait until Aitahang took the flock up to the high pasture. Do you want that to happen?' and Ama gave a heavy, wailing sigh.

As soon as the evening meal was eaten Aitahang slipped round to his father. 'Let me go with you tomorrow,' he begged.

His father looked surprised: 'Someone must stay and look after the womenfolk.'

'I'll find the tracks for you—I've been practising!'

But his mother broke in, 'You mustn't think of taking him!' and his father nodded. 'Your mother's right, you must stay with her. Now, let's get some sleep, we'll be busy tomorrow.'

But the next day was the same: a long silence, and the weary return of father and son at dusk, empty-handed.

That evening the family ate their evening meal in silence. This daily trek out after what seemed a ghost leopard could not go on. The work of the farm was being neglected, and the grazing on the lower pasture was nowhere near sufficient for the flock. Yet soon the leopard would strike again, either at dead of night or more boldly, as he had been wont to do down across the Kabeli, in broad daylight.

That night Aitahang lay long awake; he had not had too tiring a day, and he turned over and over in his mind the thought that if anyone in the family could track the leopard it was he—Aitahang of the lost goat. Yet no one in the family knew of his ability to track; he had not bothered to mention it till now, it had hardly seemed important. He was a dutiful boy, and his father's orders to stay behind had to be obeyed. Yet surely there was something that he could do to help? He lay worrying over the problem till he fell into uneasy sleep, only to awaken in the white glare of moonlight before dawn, the answer in his mind. He had been forbidden to accompany his father—but not actually to have a look by himself. He thought quickly: an hour to the top of the high pasture, then a quick look as dawn broke. He might even be able to return before he was missed, though he ruefully admitted to himself that this was unlikely. He would start at once.

He slipped out quietly, shivering in the frosty air after the cosy warmth of his bear fur in the hay, whispered to Bhalu as he stretched with a rattle of chain, and walked quietly out of the courtyard. The shadows behind the farm-house were black and menacing but he had no feeling of immediate danger, and set off uphill at a great pace, giving silent thanks for the moonlight.

Aitahang reached the top of the pasture before dawn, and spent half an hour huddled behind a rock just short of the tree-line till grey dawn came. For a moment he felt his scalp prickle; was there something in the dark woods—something unknown, mysterious yet by no means unfriendly? He had no impression that a leopard was close by, there was no feeling of danger, only of some presence . . . but the light was now strong enough to see by, the feeling vanished and he ran up to where the great fallen pine lay, at the top end of the pasture.

Almost at once he saw the double set of prints where his father and brother had begun their search on the two previous days. The remains of the goat—a gnawed skull and fragments of the carcass—were proof enough that the leopard had made a good meal, and it was not surprising that Padamlal had searched backwards and forwards in the immediate area on the first day, for such a meal would have tempted an ordinary leopard to lie up in some sheltered spot, digesting comfortably. But, admitted Aitahang, this was no ordinary leopard; normal assumptions did not apply to him—he would follow no normal rules.

Aitahang looked around, studying the ground, but in the immediate area of the fallen pine saw no leopard prints. Carefully he started again, making wider and wider casts up towards the woods, almost reaching the first trees. He saw his father's prints, and his brother's, but none of the leopard's. This puzzled him, for it was still less than three months since the end of the monsoon, and the earth, though much drier, was nothing like as dry and hard as it would become in March and April. The leopard should have left *some* spoor beyond the pine. Gradually he became convinced that the leopard had not come up this way at all. In that case, he reasoned, although it had seemed unlikely, the leopard must have turned down towards the low pasture once again.

With mounting interest he realized that again the leopard had done the unexpected. No wonder he had eluded his hunters down by the Kabeli for so long! Aitahang turned back to the fallen pine and started his search again, but this time back downhill and a little to one side. A tiny scratch on a rock, as of a claw-mark, caught his eye and he extended his search on down the same line. In half a dozen paces he came to a patch of disturbed grass, then the same distance on he found where a small stone had been moved a trifle. Gently he turned it over and there, in the damper soil underneath, were the clear imprints of round toes tipped with claw-points. He straightened up and looked along the line in which they led. It pointed down at an angle across the side of the high pasture, on past the foot of the eagle's cliff and down to the Mewa, to a spot where the river narrowed and rushed fast between giant boulders—mere stepping-stones for a leopard that could spring thirty feet. Aitahang hissed his satisfaction and bounded downhill to the farm.

At sight of him his mother's expression changed from anxiety to a flash of anger. 'Why did you go off like that!' she scolded. 'We thought the leopard might have taken you!' She had been crying, and Aitahang felt a pang of remorse until he remembered his news. 'You must have something to eat,' his mother went on, 'you must have been up since goodness knows when,' and she bustled about, but Aitahang slipped past her and said hurriedly to his father, 'I've found the tracks, the leopard didn't go into the woods, it went back down towards the river!' He was so excited that the words rushed out. 'I found its tracks by the tree, but going back down; it went down past the cliff, then on to the narrows by those big boulders, and—'

'Steady on!' interrupted his father, staring in astonishment. 'You say you found the tracks!'

'I told you, Father, I've been practising!' Aitahang was calming down and explained. 'Years ago, when I lost the goat and couldn't find it again, I swore I'd learn to track, and I did.'

'But who taught you—how did you learn?'

'I taught myself, Father.' He smiled shyly. 'It took some time.'

'Quick, Mother, feed the boy,' commanded Padamlal. He and Balahang had been ready since sun-up. 'If he's really found the tracks we must hurry.' He went to the door and stared out down to the Mewa and across to the wooded slopes beyond, while behind him Aitahang hastily swallowed mouthfuls of rice and vegetables. Once he had finished Padamlal said, 'Ready? Then we'll go.' There was no more talk of Aitahang staying at home.

The sun was well up in the morning sky when they reached the Mewa at the narrows. Just short of it Aitahang spent a few minutes searching about, for it was quite possible that the leopard had turned away from his line once again—that would have been superlatively cunning. But to his considerable relief Aitahang found a single pug-mark, clear and sharp in the damper earth above the Mewa. Padamlal and Balahang stooped to study it, then straightened up to look at the tree-line far above, then stared at Aitahang in admiration. 'Well, boy—' Padamlal clapped him on the shoulder. 'What can I say?'

'Let's just get the leopard, Father.'

Padamlal laughed, more cheerful than Aitahang had seen him for days. 'We'll get across.'

Crossing the Mewa three months after the end of the monsoon was no great hazard; it was no longer swollen with the summer rains, and the yearly rush of melted glacier water had ended in early September. But there was still enough water and strength in the current to make drowning all too likely; a real difficulty was keeping Padamlal's powder dry, and so the musket was unloaded before they struggled across, and reloaded on the far bank. 'Now, Son,' ordered Padamlal, 'find him.'

The tracks were easier on this side of the river, with its greater vegetation and the patches of big trees and bamboo. Aitahang remembered years ago hearing the hiss of a waterfall somewhere among the trees above, and thought to himself that a waterfall with its rocky surroundings, might well provide a hideout for a leopard. However, guessing was no use, he must track the leopard foot by foot until he found him. Patiently he cast out beyond the boulders of the river bank and in a few minutes was rewarded. 'He went up here,' he called, then lowered his voice abruptly. The leopard had crossed here, but there was no telling whether he had gone on uphill or whether he was lying up a few yards away, watching them.

The only thing to do was to go on—but less than a hundred feet up the slope Aitahang stopped with uplifted hand, and behind him Padamlal raised his gun. Step by cautious step Aitahang went forward, knelt down, eyes still looking ahead, and felt the ground with his hand. Then he backed away and murmured to Padamlal: 'The leopard slept here. He has only just gone.' He indicated the spot with a movement of his chin, and Padamlal looked. He could just make out a faint depression, oval in shape. 'How d'ye know he's just gone?' he whispered.

'Today is cold. That spot is warm. Besides, there is a print a yard or so beyond it, clean and new, where he stood up when he heard us coming.'

'Right,' Padamlal whispered to him, 'I'll go ahead now,' and he prepared to move on past Aitahang, but the boy stopped him with a touch, whispering, 'I'll go first and see to the tracks, Father—*you* kill the leopard!' and Padamlal acknowledged with a grim nod.

Slowly, step by step, they climbed uphill in single file, and as they went higher and higher Aitahang's suspicions crystallized into certainty: the leopard had gone into the stretch of woods around the waterfall.

They were close enough to hear the falling water distinctly, and as they entered the trees the noise grew louder. In the damper soil under the trees the leopard's pug-marks were clear, and they noted without comment the great size of the pads and the deep impression left by a heavy animal.

At last they came up through the trees to the very edge of the waterfall, a hissing torrent pouring over a rock edge into a deep pool fifty feet below. A stray shaft of sunlight pierced the tree-tops and broke into a shimmering spectrum of rainbow colours in the mist of spray, and for a moment Aitahang paused in admiration—then his eye rested on another pug-mark, and he resumed his cautious advance, climbing steeply where the leopard's tracks led up one side of the falls. Then he paused a moment, and beckoned up his father. 'The tracks turn away, across the hill-side,' he whispered, pointing. 'He's changed direction altogether!'

Aitahang knelt again and studied the pug-mark where the leopard had changed direction, then stood and breathed into his father's ear, 'It is very new.'

He led off across the slope, eyes and mind busy, in some fifty paces reaching a curve in the slope below a clump of smooth green bamboo. He walked on a pace or two, then stopped. Something was wrong. Ahead he could see the faint line of the leopard's trail across the slope, but he felt the presence of terrible danger, very close. He turned to warn his father, and as he turned he faced the bamboos close above. The danger was there.

He raised an arm to point and Padamlal, who had been watching his every movement, lifted his muzzle-loader and curled his finger round the trigger.

'Look out!' shouted Balahang from behind.

With barely a leaf rustling the leopard sprang down at them from the bamboos.

Aitahang flung himself down below the leopard's curving spring. Padamlal crouched and pulled the trigger as the tawny shape hurtled over his head. The flash-bang of the heavy charge of black powder exploded half-muffled into the white fur along the leopard's underside, and the kick of the heavy lead ball knocked it sprawling sideways, to land with a heavy scrabbling thump no more than five yards below them. The three Limbus leapt down, kukris drawn—but the leopard was twitching in its death-throes, and they watched it finally strain out, then subside, limp and bloody.

Cautiously Balahang prodded it with his kukri point, then looked up at the other two and smiled. 'Stone dead.'

# 5 THE DECISION

Just in case this leopard had a mate near by Padamlal reloaded at once, but as he rammed down powder, wadding and ball he called across to Aitahang, 'That is *your* leopard,' and Balahang echoed him: 'Your leopard, Brother.'

Aitahang said nothing. He felt no exultation, only thankfulness that the ordeal was over—and a parching thirst. They were all thirsty and tired, and before they began the hard work of skinning the leopard they walked back to the hissing cataract below the falls and drank deeply and soaked their arms to the elbow in the icy water, then climbed back across the slope to where the leopard's carcass lay. Only then, at the sight of the limp, spotted body, the bloodstained white under-fur and the gaping, open jaws showing the terrible teeth, did they really grasp that their enemy lay dead, and relief flooded over them.

'He could kill a buffalo, that *sala*!'

'He has—many times, across the Kabeli!' Then Balahang

struck his hands together: 'We must pass the news.' He turned again to Aitahang, puzzled: 'But how did you know that he was up in the bamboos—did you spot him move? That *was* a stroke of luck!' The two boys were still tense and excited from their encounter, and talked in fast, jerky phrases, till Padamlal broke in, 'Did his tracks turn up towards the bamboo? I thought you were going straight on!'

Aitahang himself was puzzled. He went back up to the tracks, studied the line he had been following and called to the others, 'His tracks *do* go on.' He studied them, then followed them on while Padamlal came behind, gun at the ready. On went Aitahang for fifty yards, then stopped and pointed. The leopard's tracks turned uphill and circled back. 'He was waiting for us, above his own trail,' said Padamlal, and Aitahang shivered suddenly. If he had not felt that prickle of the scalp the three of them would now be clawed and bleeding corpses.

'He was a devil, all right,' said Padamlal, 'but he's dead.' Then he looked about him approvingly. 'I haven't been up here before—too out of the way, but by Shiva it's a handsome spot!' He walked up and down a few paces. 'A man could build a good homestead here, with all this wood and water. And look at that bamboo! Down on the border you'd get near a rupee a length for this stuff!' He sighed. 'But it's a little remote, that's why its owner never farmed it himself.'

'Doesn't it belong to the Government?' asked Balahang. 'I thought that all this wild land did.'

'Most of it does,' replied Padamlal, 'but the old Phedangba legally bought this patch years ago, for his son. But the boy went to the war, and never returned.'

'Was he killed?'

'No one knows. There was a great battle, in a country called Ee-Ta-Lee, at a holy mountain of the Christians. Many died, and some were never found.' He sighed. 'That Phedangba is the same who cast the spells for you both when you were tiny babies, and who made the amulets you wear.'

'Perhaps,' said Aitahang slowly, 'he will sell the land to someone.'

'Perhaps. One or two have asked him, but always he said he was waiting for his son. Gradually the men from his son's regiment began coming back—those that were left—and they all said the same. So at last he accepted that his son is dead, and last year he said that he would sell.' Padamlal shrugged his shoulders. 'But who here has money to buy? This land would cost two hundred rupees an acre, and he has a good three acres. Who has that sum of money?'

The listening Aitahang sighed to himself. In the years to come he would graze his father's flock on the pasture across the Mewa and watch while some fortunate farmer with money built his house among these graceful bamboos, with water from the falls diverted to run past his door along bamboo pipes, firewood for the lifting in the woods and green grazing on the slopes above. Again he sighed, more resignedly this time. It couldn't be helped. There was nothing that a penniless shepherd boy could do, nothing at all. He plucked out his skinning knife and hurried over to help his father. 'Ama will be pleased,' he said as he squatted to work, 'and Little Sister.' Then a thought struck him and he said hesitantly, 'Father, the leopard skin—'

Padamlal, straddling the leopard and busy with his skinning knife, paused and looked up. 'Yes, Son? What about the skin? This leopard is yours.'

'Well then—Little Sister shall have it!'

As cold winter warmed into spring Aitahang found himself gazing more and more often across the Mewa to the woods and bamboo groves around the waterfall, wondering rather sadly just when he would see men cutting out a terraced site for a strong farm-house. The weeks passed, however, with no sign of work, and his father commented one evening that the spot, though attractive, well-watered and with ample wood and grazing, was remote. 'We're pretty far up,' he pointed out, 'and there's land enough for those who can pay for it much nearer the big bazaars of Taplejung and Dhankuta. So much less to carry the doko, my son.' He smiled. 'The air is good here, but the road is far!'

Aitahang nodded agreement. Each additional mountain ridge across which to carry produce and supplies meant either heavy effort for the farmer and his sons, or more money to pay porters.

'Also,' went on Padamlal, 'I heard the other day from our neighbour that the Phedangba had refused an offer from one of these Tamangs, looking for land high up. Tamangs were all very well, he said, but he would sell only to a Limbu.' He took a long breath. 'But what Limbu has six hundred rupees?'

The cold dry weather was good for walking, and as news of the death of the leopard spread, visitors began to arrive at the farm, asking to see the skin. They were mainly farmers from the valley of the Kabeli, most of them Limbus, but one or two of them Gurungs, descendants of the Western Gurkha invaders of two centuries before. All had suffered losses of cattle and goats by the leopard, and had taken time off especially to convince themselves that their hated enemy was dead. None had seen more than a glimpse of the leopard alive, however—except one man, and he bore frightful claw-marks to prove it, parallel lines running down one cheek into his neck and chest.

'I will tell you whether it is the Kabeli leopard or not,' he said as Little Sister proudly brought out the beautiful spotted fur for him to examine. 'Will you look behind its left foreleg and along its ribs?' he asked Padamlal. 'If there is a long scar there, about four years old, it is he.'

Padamlal looked but saw nothing. The scarred man heaved a sigh of disappointment. 'We had hoped it was he, when we heard,' he said sadly. 'It is long since we rested easy at night. And,' he looked gravely at Padamlal, 'you know what happens when these four-footed thieves grow old and slow.'

Padamlal nodded. 'They become man-eaters.'

'They become man-eaters. We will not know when, until one of our children does not return one day from grazing the flock.' He rose to leave, but paused. 'Huzoor,' he said. 'That scar on the leopard—it was made four years ago.'

Padamlal struck his knee. 'Of course! It will have been grown over with new fur!' The two men knelt by the outspread skin and the scarred man blew gently, ruffling up the fur the wrong way. He leant back, his anxious expression relaxed, and he showed his teeth in a fierce smile. Under the tawny, spotted fur appeared a thin white line, a long line curving from behind the left foreleg along the flank.

The family looked at him, at the deeply scarred face and back to the spotted fur, the white line again invisible, and the scarred man nodded. 'Yes—I fought him one night with my kukri. I found him in my goat-pen and waited in the doorway. He had already taken many of my animals, and this time I decided it was him or me. I struck at his head, but he was quick as lightning, drew back, then rushed me in the doorway before I could swing up my kukri to strike at him again. But I got it partly up, and though he clawed me aside as he jumped I felt the blade score along his left side as he went through the door. My wife found me: she could not tell whose was all the blood, mine or the leopard's. Later my sons found more blood in the jungle outside, though not enough for a mortal wound. He has never come back to my farm, but I have always feared for my children.' He nodded. 'And now he is dead, and you killed him. All who live by the Kabeli will be grateful.'

Padamlal reached out an arm and pulled Aitahang forward. 'Here is the one to thank. I tried for two days to find and track this leopard, and failed. But my second son here found the tracks and followed him far, finally smelling him out just as he was about to spring. Yes,' and Padamlal clapped Aitahang's shoulder, 'this is the man responsible.'

Aitahang stood awkwardly silent. The public praise embarrassed him, but he was secretly pleased by one thing: it was the first time that his father had referred to him as a man. The scarred man spoke again, this time to Aitahang and using not the familiar 'thee' affectionately used to children or to underlings, but the more straightforward 'you', as between equals—another compliment. 'What is your name, young friend?'

'Aitahang, Huzoor.'

'Well, Aitahang, we of the Kabeli will have *pujas* done by the priests for your good fortune.' He saluted Padamlal with a lift of the hand. 'My respects, Huzoor. Farewell, Aitahang, farewell, all the family.'

This praise was pleasant, but more important to Aitahang was something that he himself did not realize, although his father and mother noted it: this very real personal achievement gave him confidence in himself. Outwardly he remained much as he always had been—quiet, rather introspective, but affectionate, and somehow rather diffident about his own efforts. Now, whatever the task, from ploughing for the first time with a pair of buffaloes to having his very first shot with his father's musket, he approached it with an easy assurance.

Some weeks after the scarred man's visit Ama saw a stranger coming along the path to the farm-house, a boy of about Aitahang's age with a haversack slung from his shoulder. He greeted her respectfully and asked in Limbu Kura if this were the house of Padamlal.

'It is,' she replied. 'He is down ploughing in the terraced field, with the two sons.' She watched curiously as he thanked her and hurried down to where the menfolk were busy with the great water-buffaloes, preparing the narrow terraces for the coming rice-planting.

They stopped work when they saw the visitor. 'Someone else to see the leopard-skin?' wondered Padamlal aloud, but greeted the boy pleasantly with a cry of 'Hullo there—where have *you* sprung from?'

The boy smiled. 'From across the Kabeli, Huzoor, the son of Bhimlal,' and he drew two fingers down his right cheek. He swung round his haversack and pulled a long package from it. 'This has been sent for your second son, Huzoor.'

'Something for you, Son,' said Padamlal. Puzzled, Aitahang brushed his hands together to rid them of some of the caked, dried-on mud, and took the package.

'Open it, then!' commanded Padamlal while the stranger stood smiling. 'Let us see what he's brought!'

Although he knew as soon as he took it what the package contained, nothing had quite prepared Aitahang for what he saw when he finally unwrapped the last linen binding. It was, as he had guessed, a kukri—but a kukri such as he had never hoped to own. The scabbard was of black leather and tipped with shining steel; the gleaming blade was long, slender and balanced to perfection; and the Limbu-style handle was of buffalo-horn, the broad butt capped with a shaped steel plate. It was finer even than the one his father had admired so much in Taplejung bazaar all those years before.

The three of them stood looking at Aitahang turning the blade and balancing it in his hand. 'Many by the Kabeli contributed,' said the boy. 'That news about the leopard brought relief to the whole area.'

Later, when the young visitor had been fed and had set out on his long walk home—which he would do in a day and a half, not being burdened with a doko—and with the precious kukri re-wrapped and stowed in the family chest, Padamlal found himself thinking of many things. First, he was worried whether all this fuss might go to Aitahang's head, although he admitted there had been no sign of this so far. Next, he thought back with a sense of unease to the visit, six years earlier, of the Lama.

This was not the first time that he had pondered over that strange incident, and although he had tried to dismiss the Lama's prophecies as just shrewd guesses by an experienced traveller, yet events seemed to reveal these as rather more. That business of

Balahang falling into the river—that was likely enough to happen to any Gurkha boy who carried loads to market or who fished in the river occasionally. And the fact that a bamboo had saved him did not necessarily mean anything either; there was plenty of bamboo about, especially in the river valleys.

But the Lama had spoken of the leopard—not to him, Padamlal, but to Aitahang. How could he have known about that?

And then he had mentioned some search for 'the One-Eyed'. Could that be some dangerous animal to be hunted, that Aitahang must remember the leopard in this search? Padamlal felt that he must keep this warning in mind, but that it might be as well for Aitahang *not* to be reminded of it. He had only been seven or eight when the Lama had passed, and he had very likely forgotten all about it. Many things had happened in the interval, and he had certainly never referred to the Lama, even after pulling Balahang from the river.

In this case, Padamlal reasoned, silence was probably the best policy—it wouldn't do to worry the boy. After all, if any one-eyed animal *did* turn up, he would be there to remind Aitahang of the Lama's advice to remember the leopard, whatever that might mean. For the present, then, he would say nothing. Satisfied with his decision he dismissed the matter from his mind.

That year the monsoon arrived early, the first clouds racing west over the passes from Kangchenjunga early in May, drenching the land—much to Padamlal's satisfaction—but also shutting out from Aitahang's view the delectable stretch of pasture and woodland across the Mewa where the leopard had died. Aitahang was surprised at the intensity with which he longed to gaze on that land again; somehow he had identified himself with it, although he kept reminding himself that his growing ambition to own it was no more than the wildest of dreams. He kept these to himself, not even telling his bosom friend Manbahadur, for although he would sympathize he would only remind Aitahang of the brutal truth—that they were landless and penniless shepherd-boys who never saw a rupee from one month's end to another.

Curiously enough it was Manbahadur who raised the subject of land. He had accompanied his parents to visit a relative a little farther down the valley of the Mewa, and he mentioned to Aitahang that one of the sons had been home on leave from that unknown country Ma-la-ya.

'Is the war finished?' asked Aitahang.

'No. He says it will be long,' replied Manbahadur. They were sitting sheltering from the rain in the sheep-pen, while steam from the damp, curly fleeces rose round them.

'I'll be glad when this monsoon ends,' commented Aitahang. The sheep-pen was deep in trampled mud and droppings, while outside the earth paths and courtyard were little more than a muddy porridge, churned up by the huge hoofs of the water-buffaloes. He took out his working kukri and began carefully to scrape blobs of mud from his bare legs.

'This soldier,' said Manbahadur returning to the subject, 'has a watch. It cost forty rupees.'

Aitahang stopped scraping and stared in disbelief. Manbahadur nodded. 'It is quite true. But more than that, he has bought two acres, and says that the next time he comes on leave, in three years' time, he will be able to buy even more!' He sighed wistfully. 'If I had land I could build a house.'

'We will each get our share eventually, by inheritance.'

'It is long to wait.'

They sat in silence, listening to the drumming rain and watching the rainwater lash itself into a yellow froth in the deep muddy holes of the buffalo footprints. As the chill of evening closed in, the mist thickened, Manbahadur hastily set off for home and Aitahang set about the evening's chores—splitting firewood, making the sheep-pen secure, seeing to the buffaloes, feeding Bhalu, cleaning the working tools—a seemingly endless sequence of jobs. That night, when the mist closed in, condensing in heavy droplets on the sodden thatch and even dampening the bear's fur around him, he lay long awake, thinking. Later he slept, but only fitfully, and awoke early, his mind made up. He would go to the war to earn money for the land.

He broached the subject delicately two or three weeks later when he met Manbahadur, and the older boy said knowingly, 'You're set on going, aren't you!'

Thus confronted, Aitahang admitted that he was.

'Well,' said Manbahadur, 'I'll come too.'

# 6 GALLA

Aitahang did not sleep a wink the night before he left. Every half-hour after midnight he peered out at the moon, full and clear in the cloudless night sky, the monsoon just past. At last, when he reckoned it was two hours before dawn, he slipped down from the hayloft, still wrapped in his fur, whispered to Bhalu and entered the farm-house. He opened the family chest, took out his new kukri and closed the lid carefully. Then he folded the fur, laid it on top of the box and laid his working kukri on top of that. This was the only way he could leave word that he had gone of his own free will. He could not have told his parents earlier; they would have forbidden him to go, and would have extracted his promise that he would not.

For a moment he stood in the darkness of the lower room, the familiar scent of pine-wood in his nostrils, hearing from outside the sounds of cattle shifting in the byre, and the clink of Bhalu's chain. Through a crack in the window boards he saw moonlight glitter on the snows of Topke, and impulsively he stretched out his hand to the lid of the chest again, tempted to replace his new kukri and steal back to the hayloft beside his brother. No one would ever know.

But he conquered his impulse. It was too late to draw back, and besides, Manbahadur was waiting. With a resolute movement he thrust the new fighting kukri into his cummerbund, stepped outside carefully, bent down and hugged Bhalu. 'I will return,' he whispered. 'Guard them well for me.'

A mile along the path Manbahadur was waiting. 'All right?' he whispered.

'All right. Everything quiet.'

'The *galla* meets beyond Changa at sun-up. We must hurry.'

Lightly clad and without any load the two boys sped along the path, crossed the slope and hurried down to the river, crossed the cantilever bridge with caution and ran on again. Soon after dawn they were in Changa—a few houses scattered across the slope above the river. The boys slowed down, panting, and looked about them anxiously. 'I don't see anyone,' panted Aitahang, his chest heaving. He wiped the sweat from his eyes and drew a deep, shaky breath. Dawn was well past, the sun was just clearing the east ridge and there was no sign of the *galla*. By now his father would have found the folded fur, and would know where he had gone. He would be certain to follow this far at least. Again Aitahang felt a stab of remorse, but he said determinedly, 'Let's look a bit farther on.' They set off again at a run and round a bend in the path blundered into a group of fifteen or so lads squatting in silence against the hill-side. A middle-aged man, his face half-hidden in a twisted muffler, came up to them and said hastily in Limbu Kura, 'You two coming?'

'Coming, Huzoor,' affirmed Manbahadur.

'Good.' The recruiter looked anxious. 'Seen any others on the way?'

'No one.'

'Very well, then. That must be all.' He turned to speak to the group, changing to Gurkhali. 'Does everyone understand what I say?'

'We understand, Huzoor,' called one or two, while others nodded.

Aitahang looked at his companions. By the kukris and their looks he could tell that most were Limbus, one or two of the others were Gurungs and two looked like Buddhist Tamangs.

'Listen,' the recruiter went on hurriedly, 'I can only take twelve—' there was a startled silence—'I may only bring twelve lads to the recruiting centre; any more with me will not be allowed past the gate.' The boys exchanged worried glances. 'I will measure you all, and those who are not big enough, or who are too old or too young must go home. I will do that now so that they can get home quickly.' He knew well enough that most had come without permission. 'Right, we'll start.'

Aitahang felt his heart sink. He would be bound to be sent back as too young—that recruiter was no fool. He watched anxiously as one by one the others were summoned and measured against the recruiter's long staff. Those of the correct height he looked at critically, and at one or two he shook his head, saying, 'Too old, your muscles have set.'

They protested, saying, 'We are strong, Huzoor, we will work hard!' But he repeated, 'Your muscles have set. The Recruiting Sahib only takes those who are still green, like growing saplings.' At this Aitahang felt a twinge of hope, but when his turn came to stand against the staff he trembled so much that the recruiter said, 'Take it easy, lad—take it easy.' He looked at the staff: 'Your height is all right,' then looked Aitahang up and down. 'I'm not so sure about your age; you look a bit young to me. How old are you?'

'Seventeen, Huzoor,' said Aitahang desperately.

'No, no—you can tell the Sahib that, but tell me the truth.'

'Fourteen, Huzoor—fifteen after the Dasehra festival.'

'H'm, that's more like it.' The recruiter looked at him again, doubtfully, then said, 'Wait to one side.'

He next measured Manbahadur, looked him up and down and sent him farther along the path to join those who had passed. Aitahang was racked with anxiety. It had never occurred to him that he might not be taken—or that he and Manbahadur might be separated. The recruiter now had eleven, and there was still one young lad to look at, but the recruiter shook his head. 'Too short by half an inch—but you're young; by next year you'll be tall enough and I'll take you then!' The boy nodded with a glum face and set off back along the path at a run. The recruiter turned to Aitahang: 'I'll take you along, but you mustn't be disappointed if the Recruiting Sahib rejects you as too young.'

'All right.'

'Right, then, let's get out of here.' The recruiter had no wish to be caught up by indignant parents, and led off along a side path at a fast walk. From now on, Aitahang realized, it would be hard walking along difficult by-paths till they reached the border.

At halts for rest the aspiring soldiers exchanged guarded confidences, mainly a probing for family relationships. Many recognized each other, and most had come in pairs. All were farmers' sons, and many had relatives who had served in the army. Two were younger brothers of men still serving, and one, the proud possessor of a velvet waistcoat, confided that his father had retired as a Captain. He was the only son, he said, but his father had let him go. He would be the fifth in line to serve in that Regiment.

After the first scatter of talk the lads concentrated on keeping up with the fast pace set by the recruiter, and saved their breath. Not till nightfall did they halt, at a lonely farm-house far down the Mewa, where they were obviously expected, for a meal of rice and fish was waiting for them. The twelve were almost too weary to eat. All had been up since well before dawn, they had walked and run miles to the rendezvous, had experienced the tension of the first rough selection by the recruiter, and had walked fast all day with a few halts for rest and none for food. As soon as they had eaten they huddled together for warmth and fell asleep to the hypnotic roaring of the river below—still in full spate after the months of rain.

The next morning came tragedy. Crossing the Mewa by another of the dangerous bridges, this time a sagging affair of cross-sticks between two ropes with a slack wire handrail swinging somewhere above it, part of the bridge broke under the weight of one of the twelve. He plunged straight down, the jerk tore his grip from the wire handrail and he vanished into the foaming water below. He did not reappear and though the recruiter and the others ran downstream as fast as they could to try and intercept him, he was not seen again. It was the Captain's son.

Grim-faced, the recruiter hurried back to the house where

they had spent the night and arranged that news be sent to the drowned boy's home, then returned and led the eleven on again, uphill.

It was a day Aitahang would not forget. Delayed by the tragedy their long climb up to the ridge of the Kangchenjunga foothills which marked the border was not completed before darkness, and they sheltered that night in an empty, half-collapsed hut used for the summer grazing by the shepherds of the region. There was water, but no food, their height was over ten thousand feet and the cold was bitter. Numb and faint with hunger they marched on again the next morning, climbing another two thousand feet to the ridge of Phalelung.

Just short of it Aitahang looked back west. Behind him in the crystal air half the world seemed to be snow peaks and glaciers, the great black pyramid standing back from, yet higher than them all. At the sight of that vista, like a glimpse of eternity, he felt his present pain and discomfort as of little account—and there, on the crest not far above was the recruiter, calling down, 'The border, lads!'

The crest line itself was grown with a scattering of thin woods on its eastern edge, and the group could see nothing till they reached a gap, then saw below them the huge drop to the valley of the Rungeet, with beyond the hills of Darjeeling backed by yet more mountains.

'We're heading for Jalapahar, a thousand feet above Darjeeling,' the recruiter told them. 'We'll reach it this afternoon. But we'll have something to eat at this first little bazaar ahead, Daragaon, a mile or two down the hill path.'

Tucked into the shelter of the ridge some three thousand feet below, Daragaon was a one-street village of shops selling cloth and other supplies, and inns selling food and liquor. At one of these the recruiter bargained briefly for a meal for them all, agreed on price and quantity with the innkeeper and motioned to the lads to seat themselves at the rough wooden benches in the open front portion. Farther inside, in a screened-off room, Aitahang heard a a low hum of talk and a drunken voice upraised, and smelt rice spirit. Casually the recruiter said, 'Stay together, lads, whenever you're in these border villages—they're full of robbers and all sorts of low characters.' Aitahang and Manbahadur glanced at each other: this wasn't exactly what they had expected to find.

Along the street lounged two or three idle-looking fellows in hill clothing, but without the lean, rather worn look of the real hillman. Instead these looked sluggish and rather pasty, with a sullen yet insolent air about them. Busy popping handfuls of rice into his mouth Aitahang eyed them: had they no work to do, no flocks to tend? How did they exist if they just hung around the bazaar? There was one big fellow in particular—he looked as if he should be able to carry a two-hundredweight doko all day, earning double rates, yet here he was, loafing, chewing betel-nut and spitting great streams of scarlet juice over the street. Aitahang dismissed him from his mind, and finished the last of his rice and vegetables, feeling warmer and better for the hot food.

'All finished, lads?' The recruiter counted them as they gathered in the street. 'We'll go, then.'

Down and down they went, down into the huge valley, through increasing numbers of larger and larger villages, at the valley-bottom coming for the first time to slopes covered with shoulder-high bushes. 'Tea,' said the knowing ones, 'look at the quantity of it!' Everywhere on the far, rising slopes were tea gardens, the bushes in carefully terraced rows, and men and women working among them. Some paused to call out to the party, '*Lahurey Dzahnay?*' but apart from a brief 'Ho!' of confirmation and a wave or two of the hand the youngsters went on without pausing. With their goal now only a few thousand feet above them they were not disposed to stop and chat.

By mid-afternoon they had reached Darjeeling, climbing up into it through a shanty-town inhabited, to Aitahang's complete astonishment, by Tibetans and others he recognized as Sherpas. By now he was quite overwhelmed with the rush of new sights and impressions, so much so that his first motor-car, honking busily as it drove through bigger crowds than he had even seen before, drew from him no more than a casual glance. Even when Manbahadur goggled down at a great black iron machine puffing clouds of steam and pulling at least a dozen little carriages with people leaning out of the windows he only looked and nodded, 'Oh, yes—my father used to tell me of those.' His mind was set only on the stone barracks perched on the ridge a thousand feet above.

A short while later the commander of the quarter-guard at the Recruiting Depot heard a call from the sentry, '*Galla ayo!*' and telephoned up the hill to the Recruiting Officer. 'Another *galla* coming up, Huzoor,' he announced, and the Recruiting Officer put on his cap, buckled on his Sam Browne belt and strode down the hill to meet them, followed by the Depot Quartermaster with his guides.

As he stood in the growing wind of late afternoon, glad of his warm battle-dress uniform, watching the file of barefoot, shock-headed youngsters climb the last few hundred feet of ridge road, the Recruiting Officer heard a passing coolie cry out to them, '*Lahurey Dzahnay?*' and nodded recognition. This ancient cry, meaning 'To Lahore do you go?' dated back over the centuries to when penniless Gurkhas owning nothing but courage and a kukri made the long journey west to Lahore in the Punjab, to sell their services for the princely wars—in Gilgit, in Kashmir, in Sind, in Leh; against the Tibetans, against the Chinese, against the Baluchis and the Pathans—to anyone who would pay; all long before the rule of law brought to the area by the British. Lahore was the market-place for mercenaries. Many a Gurkha farm was bought with rupees from the princes of Hindustan, but many a Gurkha mother never saw her son again. So, up in the Gurkha hills the name Lahore, corrupted to Lahurey, became synonymous with military service.

As they drew nearer the Recruiting Officer recognized the recruiter as Jagatman Limbu, formerly a sergeant in the 10th Gurkhas and a pensioner since the war, now earning a little extra money bringing in recruits. Jagatman halted his group, arranged them in a rough line and reported: 'Eleven lads, Huzoor.'

The Recruiting Officer nodded. They looked a good bunch—one or two a trifle young; these might have to be sent back to wait another year. 'You didn't get your twelve, then?' he asked.

'Lost one, Huzoor, crossing the Mewa.'

The officer did not ask for elaboration of that curt statement. He could well visualize the scene—the rickety bridge, the foaming torrent, the fall, the desperate attempts at rescue. 'Where did the boy come from?'

'Maiwa Khola. He was the son of Captain Bhimprasad, First Battalion.'

'Went on pension just after the war?'

'The same.'

The Recruiting Officer was silent for a moment. If only the boy had stayed at home—then again, he might well have died there of fever, or in a mountain avalanche, or in any of a dozen ways. Life was hazardous in the hills. 'Tomorrow rest your lads,' he ordered. 'We're looking at two *gallas* from Tehra Thum at the moment. We'll start on yours the day after tomorrow.'

Jagatman saluted and the Quartermaster and his team took over. First the group was led to the store, where each man was issued with two blankets, a mess-tin and a mug. Next they were taken to the cookhouse, where soldiers of the Depot were already filing past receiving their evening meal. 'Come back for more, lads,' called the cooks as they issued great ladlefuls of rice and split peas and mutton, 'plenty here!' The youngsters gulped it all down hungrily, then rather doubtfully approached the cooks again, who called out, 'Don't be shy!' and filled their mess-tins again.

All the next day Jagatman's *galla* rested, eating enormously of the two main meals, having hair-cuts and hot showers, and the rest of the time wandering about the stone barracks, admiring the silent sentries in their battle-dress and rifle-green berets with silver badges and rows of medal ribbons, and listening to bugle calls. Sometimes Aitahang was seized with doubt: would he ever become one of these stocky, sunburnt men in their warm clothing and heavy boots? For a while the group watched the incomprehensible activities going on all over the broad parade-ground. Two other groups of youngsters, wearing only G-strings, were being weighed and measured and looked at and questioned, while uniformed Gurkha clerks filled in forms and wrote on long sheets of paper. It was all very confusing.

In the middle of it all stood the Recruiting Officer. His purpose in life was recruiting—he found it fascinating, yet he hated it, for always at the end of the day he had to fail young men for trivial reasons, simply because there were more recruits than places. Each year he longed for the recruiting season to end, so that he could finish with the harsh business of telling nearly half of those who came that they must return home again. This he did curtly and quickly; he could hardly bear the look in their eyes.

The next two days were for Aitahang days of strain and apprehension. He was weighed and measured; his teeth and ears were examined; his chest was listened to by a British officer with tubes from his ears; Gurkha officers ordered him to run up and down the parade-ground and watched his movements critically; his hands were looked at, to see if he could open and close his fingers properly—'You must be able to squeeze a trigger, Boy,' he was told; his eyesight was tested and his feet closely examined, and at the end of the second day, with Jagatman in close attendance, his group and two others, about forty lads in all, were formed into a long line. This, they were told, was the first selection of those who had passed the physical tests. After this the Recruiting Sahib would make the final choice.

Now the tension mounted and the youngsters stood still as stone, each wrapped in a blanket till a Gurkha officer tapped him on the shoulder, when he dropped it and stood stiffly to attention, naked but for a G-string.

Aitahang could see from the corner of his eye the Gurkha officer coming down the line, all too often ordering one of the youngsters to step back into the second line, the line for those the Gurkha officers did not recommend. Manbahadur was left standing in the front rank, and then the Gurkha officers reached Aitahang. His shoulder was tapped, he dropped his blanket and stood still, drawing himself up as much as he could. The senior Gurkha officer looked at him a long moment, then with a rough kindness said, 'Too young, lad—try again next year,' and pushed him back.

Picking up his blanket Aitahang stepped back into the second line, his heart heavy as lead. Tomorrow he would be paid travelling allowances and sent home again, in the group of those that had not been taken. His parents would welcome him—but he would feel their unspoken reproaches, and he would return to tending his flock on the high pasture, and gazing across the Mewa at the land which would never be his. He barely noticed that the Recruiting Officer himself was now coming down the line.

At last he came to Aitahang, and paused. 'Too young, Sahib,' said the senior Gurkha officer, 'but we could take him next year.'

The Recruiting Officer nodded, but did not move on immediately. Here was a potentially very good recruit: he could see that by the set of his head and his calm gaze. Aitahang in turn looked up at the Recruiting Officer, still intrigued by the light eyes and the greater height of these Sahibs. The Recruiting Officer mused to himself: here was a youngster, a Limbu by the look of him, probably run away from home to join, and unlike others in the second row—some a trifle old and set, others with some slight fault of posture or appearance—this boy's only fault was youth. But perhaps it would be as well to agree with the Gurkha officer's recommendations and send him back, with instructions to return next year. He was about to nod and move on when his eye was caught by an amulet the boy was wearing round his neck, a small container of stitched leather on a cord. He looked from the amulet to the calm, trusting eyes, and felt something stir within him—compassion, perhaps—and with a swift movement tapped Aitahang on the shoulder, ordered 'Front rank', and moved on to the next man.

The rest of the day passed for Aitahang like a wonderful dream. He and Manbahadur and the others accepted were placed in single file before a table and asked if they had connections with any particular Regiment. Greatly daring Aitahang called out, 'Let me and Manbahadur go to the same Regiment!' and the Gurkha officer laughed and said, 'Very well.' So they were given numbers in sequence: Manbahadur became 22136612 Rifleman Manbahadur Limbu, and Aitahang became 22136613 Rifleman Aitahang Limbu, both of the 10th Princess Mary's Own Gurkha Rifles. Their last four numbers were then painted on their chests with gentian violet from the doctor's medical chest and each man was individually photographed, again wearing only a G-string.

It was explained to them that from now on they must expect to be identified by their regimental numbers, and addressed by their seniors by the last two numbers. 'We can't go about calling you Second Son, or Elder Son or Middle Son, now—can we?' chaffed the Gurkha officer who was explaining things to them. 'Nor can we call you, say, Manbahadur Limbu, or Balbahadur Rai. Hands up all the Manbahadur Limbus!' and to surprised laughter no less than nine youngsters held their hands up. 'You see? But numbers are all different!'

The new recruits laughed again. They were all in high spirits, full of the sudden joy of release from great tension. They were next taken to the stores to be issued with uniforms, and spent a glorious hour with an N.C.O. there, trying on all sorts of unfamiliar items of clothing—underwear, long trousers, flannel shirts, jerseys, socks and finally boots. The Recruiting Officer stood watching and smiling: he always reckoned this to be the best part of recruiting—all were happy and for a while he felt like a military Father Christmas. He was always surprised by the large boot sizes the recruits took, and had to remind himself that this was caused by a barefoot life in the Himalayas, resulting in feet with heavily developed muscles and broad soles; in a few months of wearing boots these feet would get smaller and smaller, and the boot sizes would dwindle from six or seven to four or five.

'So now I call you "Twelve"!' said Aitahang to Manbahadur as they moved about trying to stop feeling clumsy in their heavy leather boots.

'And you're "Thirteen"!' replied Manbahadur with a laugh. 'You will have to get used to it, you know!'

'Yes, we must practise,' acknowledged Aitahang. So now he was just a number—the thought was a trifle daunting. But if it applied to everyone in the Gurkha Brigade it must be all right! There was something about the number thirteen, however, something that took him far back into his childhood. Someone, he thought, had mentioned it to him particularly . . . He shook his head. He must be imagining things.

For the recruits life now became a whirl of movement. A day or two after they were sworn in they were taken in trucks to the little station of Ghum Pahar, just below the Depot, where carriages were waiting for them. Then began an exciting journey by rail down the hill line to Siliguri, where they waited in the heat of the plains for a much larger train. There followed a peculiarly unpleasant journey to Calcutta, when they sweated in the heat and stared astonished at the swarming millions filling the streets. A night at a transit camp followed, then they were taken to the docks and embarked on a ship, settling down on the lower decks with blanket and groundsheet and mosquito net. The ship sailed and they hung over the rails staring at the brown of the Hooghly river till it widened and turned blue, and they were at sea.

At last, after days of sea-sickness, they reached the island of Penang, and dropped anchor in the harbour. After the crowded cities of India the sight of green palms, white buildings, order and cleanliness was doubly welcome.

'So this is Ma-la-ya,' said Aitahang as the recruits lined the ship's rails. 'It looks good.'

'And see,' said Manbahadur, pointing, 'there are mountains here too!'

# 7 AMBUSH

'Respected Father,' wrote Aitahang, 'by the grace of God and of Pashupatinath, all here is well.'

He sat back for a moment, admiring the regular lines of Nagri script on the white paper, remembering that until not so long ago his letters home had been written for him by one of the Depot instructors.

'Please pay my respects to Ama, and give my love to Elder Brother and Little Sister, and stroke Bhalu for me.'

The long barrack-room hut where he sat was nearly empty. Manbahadur and the rest of their squad of recruits were engaged in an impromptu basketball game on the floodlit court at the edge of the parade-ground, and their shouts and laughter came faintly to him through the quiet, tropical night.

'Today,' he wrote, 'we recruits completed our training, and we are now soldiers.'

Pen in hand he sat thinking over the last eight, very full months of training, months which had been much less of an ordeal than the recruits had expected. The early weeks had been spent in drill and the simplest military exercises, and only very gradually were they introduced to the more complicated business of handling and firing their weapons—rifles, sub-machine-carbines, light machine-guns, grenades and two-inch mortars—and studying section tactics. They learnt to use map and compass, listened to lectures on the histories of the Gurkha regiments and also learned to read and write, first in the Nagri script, and later in Basic English. They had also been fed extra rations to build up their growing bodies—milk and butter and eggs and cheese—to supplement the usual meat, fish and rice of their staple diet.

The culmination of their period of training was the passing-out parade, when they marched past the General of the Brigade of Gurkhas, their uniforms immaculate and their weapons gleaming. When they dismissed they were recruits no longer, but trained soldiers, the next day to set off to join one or other of the half-dozen Gurkha battalions engaged up and down Malaya in forest warfare with the Communists.

He smiled as he thought of the little ceremony held not long after the passing-out parade. A day or two earlier all the recruits had been photographed wearing only G-strings. Today they were shown these photographs, pasted in an enormous record book that held their details. But opposite this photograph was another, one that they had all forgotten about, the photograph taken just after they had been accepted as recruits. The new soldiers gasped and laughed as they compared the two photographs, and Aitahang remembered his own astonishment. The earlier showed a rather thin, pale young boy in a G-string, with his regimental number painted on his chest in gentian violet, standing stiffly and looking with defiant suspicion at the camera. This new photograph showed a youngster still boyish-looking, but a good twenty pounds heavier and three inches taller, with sunburnt face, arms and shoulders, his expression relaxed and faintly smiling. The pictures might have been of two different people.

'. . . we are now soldiers.' He bent over his letter again, forming the curving script with care. 'Tomorrow, the fourth day of August, we leave for our battalions. I go, and so does my friend Manbahadur, to the 1st Battalion 10th Gurkha Rifles, at a place called Bentong.'

So much for the news and salutations, he decided. Now he would come to the important part of the letter, to something he had as yet not mentioned to his father. 'I have saved eighty rupees from my recruit's pay,' he wrote, 'and I am sending it home with this letter by hand of a soldier whose home is near Lingten. He will deliver it to you when he goes on leave this dry season. Please keep thirty rupees for the family and take fifty rupees to the old Phedangba. Tell him that I wish to buy his land, and that I will continue to send money until the price is paid.'

He sat reading the letter over for mistakes, then signed it with further expressions of respect. He had earlier received a letter from Padamlal in which his father philosophically accepted that his son had only done what so many Gurkhas had done before him, and had left home to be a soldier. In the end, thought Aitahang, his father would really be pleased, especially if he bought the land.

Carefully he sealed the letter and took it to the soldier who was to deliver it, one of the Depot instructors due for leave. 'I have asked for the money to be given to you at Jalapahar, when you draw your own pay for leave,' he said, and the other nodded. This was the accepted method for soldiers to send money home—in the Gurkha hills there was no other way.

There—it was begun. He had taken the first step in acquiring the land. He still had much money to save, but his pay as a soldier would be more than as a recruit, and as he neither smoked nor drank he would be able to put aside a fair number of rupees each month. His heart light, he ran off to join the others.

The next morning the four hundred new soldiers set off. Of these no less than forty were in the draft for the 1st Battalian 10th Gurkhas, and Aitahang and Manbahadur stood on parade with them, in full marching order, packs on, rifles slung and kitbags stacked. Aitahung wore slung from his webbing belt a Government issue kukri; his own treasured Limbu kukri was carefully wrapped and packed in his kitbag—he was not going to expose it to the rough wear that kukris would get on operations, and besides, it was of a markedly different shape, unsuitable for parades and inspections. He could not visualize himself using it, it was too precious, but it was a link with home.

The train journey south carried the young soldiers along the west flank of the massive chain of mountains running along the spine of Malaya. 'Plenty of cover for Communists in there,' murmured Aitahang, half to himself and half to Manbahadur beside him. What would it be like, hunting men in that forest? The comparison jumped into his mind: it would be very like going after that leopard.

Hour after hour he gazed out at the huge stretches of thick country and the towering peaks and deep valleys while the others dozed or played cards. One draft left the train at Ipoh for the 2nd Battalion 2nd Goorkhas; the train rattled on again, then at last the outskirts of a big town flashed past and there were shouts of 'Get ready, First-Tenth party—Kuala Lumpur!' and the train drew clanking to a halt in a big, covered station.

Humped with pack and kitbag the draft detrained and squeezed in single file through the press of Chinese, Malays, Tamils and Europeans who thronged the platform. A Gurkha officer in faded jungle green uniform was waiting for them, and as he led them to a group of lorries Aitahang noted his well-worn webbing equipment, hung with roughly stitched canvas pouches holding carbine magazines, an automatic carbine of unfamiliar type slung from his shoulder.

'Fall in three ranks!' ordered the Gurkha officer. Quickly he checked their names against a list. As he answered Aitahang felt that he really was part of a Gurkha regiment at last.

'Stand-at—ease! Stand easy!' ordered the officer. There was a pause for a moment, and Aitahang looked around him as the draft relaxed. The vehicles waiting for them were two open three-ton lorries and a Lynx armoured scout car with bren gun mounted. He stared curiously at the half-dozen soldiers of the escort. They looked very different from the sleek instructors of the Depot; these men were dusty, their faces thinner and unusually pallid, as if they did not often see the sun. One or two, he noticed, could have done with a haircut. Then the Gurkha officer called them up to attention again.

'Listen, please,' he said, 'you all learnt ambush drill at the Depot, but I'll repeat the essentials.' His voice sounded bored, but it carried a chilling conviction. 'Before embussing charge magazines, load, and apply safety catches. Face outwards during the journey and don't bunch up in the trucks more than you have to. If we're ambushed, get out while the escort throw smoke grenades, then try to get up round behind the ambushers. Any questions?'

There were no questions, and N.C.O.s split the draft into two groups, and each was ordered to load rifles and embus. Aitahang found himself in the second lorry. 'O.K., lads?' asked the N.C.O. casually. 'Grab your kitbags and climb up.' He nodded to them reassuringly. 'We'll be in Bentong in three hours.'

'Three hours!' exclaimed one of the draft. The N.C.O. smiled.

'It's over that first lot of mountain. The rifle companies are over beyond the next!'

The road led north out of Kuala Lumpur and ran for some miles along a plain, among Malay kampongs, bamboo groves and rows of rubber trees, then turned at a junction east up into the mountains, and began to climb steeply. This was ambush country, Aitahang recognized: the road rose winding round the slopes with a steep earth bank on one side as much as twenty feet high, and on the other a sharp drop down the mountain-side. There were endless series of hairpin bends, and in the steeper spots the soldiers were able to look down on the heads of the others in the lorry behind. For nearly two hours the lorries ground uphill in low gear, finally squeezing through a narrow pass at the highest point. Aitahang saw how the escorting men's eyes turned from one side to the other, and one near him called into his ear above the engine noise, 'The Genting Sempak Pass—we've been ambushed here several times!'

Aitahang felt a surge of excitement; perhaps he was going to see action quicker than he realized—but there was no outbreak of firing, and the small convoy turned downhill without incident.

They were now travelling north-east, and at places where the forest had been cut back from the road the Gurkhas had intermittent glimpses of the vastness of Central Pahang—broad valleys, superb peaks, a great blue mountain massif farther north with its higher crests patched with cloud—all covered densely with forest, with here and there the glitter of rivers. It was wonderful country

—and a guerrilla's dream. Each time they reached an open space Aitahang felt his gaze fasten on that central mountain massif: that was where he would have his base if he were a guerrilla!

But the convoy was descending steadily, the view was lost, and in the third hour from Kuala Lumpur they reached Bentong in its mountain-girt plain.

Battalion H.Q., a big wooden house in a shady compound just outside the town of Bentong, was a busy place. Signallers stripped to the waist sat at big wireless sets in the ground-floor rooms, receiving reports from the rifle companies, and lorries and armoured scout cars came and went. Aitahang saw a British officer glance out of an upstairs window and give them a welcoming wave, then there were shouts of 'Debus! Fall in!', once again their names were checked and at last they were dismissed. 'Get some tea from H.Q. Company cookhouse,' they were told, 'but be ready to fall in again in half an hour, when you will be allotted to rifle companies.'

Shyly the recruits stayed together as they sipped their mugs of hot tea, watching the busy men around them. One or two of the older soldiers called out to them as they passed, one in Limbu Kura. 'Anyone from Dhankuta Province?' When twenty hands shot up he asked, 'From Tumling village of Tehra Thum?' and two men shouted, 'We are!' and the three of them shook hands. 'I know you two,' said the soldier, 'and your parents!' and they began to talk eagerly of home. Aitahang watched rather sadly: it was not very likely that he'd meet anyone from so remote an area as the upper Mewa. However, at least he had Manbahadur with him.

At intervals more small groups of vehicles arrived and halted on the road by Battalion H.Q. 'From the rifle companies,' said someone, 'ration convoys. You'll be going off to your companies in one of these.' The soldiers escorting each convoy turned into fatigue parties, and while they loaded up their vehicles with fresh vegetables, sacks of dry rations and the company mail, the recruits were fallen in again. An N.C.O. clerk read out the company to which each man had been allotted, and Aitahang found himself and Manbahadur in the group of six recruits posted to B Company.

A colour-sergeant with a narrow black moustache collected the B Company group. 'We'll go at once,' he told them. 'B Company is the farthest away.' Without further ceremony he ordered, 'Check your weapons! You first three—that front vehicle; next three the one behind. Now, keep alert!' and as they scrambled in he waved to the drivers to start up. 'Everyone ready? Let's go.'

The vehicles were not the large three-tonners, but smaller, handier Dodge 15-cwt trucks, their canopies stripped off as usual. Leading was an armoured Lynx scout car, a bren gun sticking out of its open top. The convoy picked up speed as it swung out of Bentong, travelling first south to the edge of the town then turning east at a big T-junction.

'How long will it take us to reach our company base?' Aitahang asked the nearer of the two escorting soldiers in the truck.

'Another two hours,' replied the soldier. 'There's a bit of a hill section we go through, and the road is narrow and not very good.'

Again Aitahang noted the man's pallor and his rather worn appearance. 'Any bandits down there?' he asked diffidently, and the soldier replied with a faint smile, 'A few.'

Aitahang chatted briefly with Manbahadur, but it was difficult to talk easily; the trucks were travelling fast, the engines were noisy and they had to cling on tight to keep their seats. For some miles they raced along a flat road between mixed forest, rubber and head-high belukar jungle. Over these low patches Aitahang caught another glimpse to the north of the blue mountain massif, and he plucked the sleeve of the soldier, and pointed: 'What's that big mountain area up there?'

The soldier called back, 'That's Gunong Benom,' and turned back to scanning the sides of the road. Soon they passed through a one-street village of Chinese shophouses—'Karak!' shouted one of the escort—and turned south at a fork on to a winding road with jungle high up on one side and a foaming river on the other, visible only occasionally below them through the screening trees and bamboos growing out above it. They were entering the hill section.

All this travelling was beginning to have its effect on Aitahang and he felt his eyes pricking with weariness. He'd be glad to reach B Company; it must be late afternoon; they'd been on the go since sunrise. He took a deep breath to revive himself, and tried to concentrate on the dense forest above the road. He could see that the others were just as sleepy, Manbahadur blinking occasionally and the other young soldier with them looking very drowsy. Only the escorts looked unwearied. Above them and around them were trees and yet more trees, crowding in on each other, overlapping so that wherever they looked there seemed to be a wall of trunks, except where the road swung out and curved above the gorge of the river.

The vehicles swung into what looked like the longest and sharpest hairpin yet. The road ran above a ravine into the hill-side and out again, a ravine so narrow that as his vehicle entered the bend Aitahang found himself looking into the goggled, dusty faces of the scout car driver and his bren-gunner coming out of the bend on the far side.

Aitahang was suddenly wide awake. This was a nasty little corner! His eyes narrowed and he rested his thumb on the safety catch of his rifle. He felt a prickle in the scalp at the back of his head and a sudden urgent sensation of danger from the slope above. He leant forward to speak to the soldier next to him when a ripple of flashes sparkled down at them from the slope, the soldier clutched at his chest and Aitahang felt a hammer-blow behind his right shoulder and was knocked sprawling in a confusion of bullets and splintering wood. The truck lurched into the ditch and drove juddering along for a few yards, the wild roaring of the engine half-drowned by the shattering uproar of rifle and automatic fire at close range. Aitahang struggled up, but the front wheels of the truck twisted round and it stopped abruptly. He was jerked out and over the right-hand side, landing heavily in the ditch and partly under the truck, where he lay bleeding and shaken.

From below the truck he caught a glimpse of the scout car. It did not follow the road round, but drove straight on. The engine raced, there was a snapping of branches, a moment of silence then a loud crash as a ton of armoured vehicle plunged into the river below.

On the road by his own truck the soldier who had sat next to him lay motionless. The driver's boots stuck out beyond the driving seat and farther on another body, unidentifiable from where he lay, was sprawled by the front wheels. Bullets still clanged into the trucks but the noise was diminishing and the firing began to die down. Painfully he realized that the Gurkhas had not fired a shot. He twisted his head round, but could see little beyond the tilted underside of the truck, the edge of the ditch by his head, the bodies on the road and the rear end of the other truck, sticking out from the culvert at the bend. There was no sign of life around it.

He felt blood spreading across the front of his shirt, and put up a hand to try to locate the wound. He found that a bullet had punched right through below his right collar-bone. He began to feel a steady, numbing ache, and realized that he must do something to stop the loss of blood. He fumbled for the field dressing in its little pocket on the thigh of his trousers, then realized he could not wind the bandage round himself without assistance—and everyone else was dead.

He let his head fall back against the bottom of the ditch. The firing had stopped, but he felt little concern. Instead, he wondered hazily if any had survived—and Manbahadur, who had sat next him, where was he? In the silence he heard a slight scrape, as of a boot moving on floorboards, and a murmur from above him. With an effort he croaked up, 'Who is it—are you hit?' There was a bump and a mutter, 'Hard hit . . .' It was Manbahadur's voice, distorted by pain.

'Can you get down?' he croaked up again, but Manbahadur only mumbled incoherently.

For a minute or two nothing seemed to be happening; there was no more shooting, and no sound except for a groaning mutter from Manbahadur. Then Aitahang heard a voice calling in Chinese.

The voice called cautiously, another voice answered, there was a pause, the sound of rustling branches and then the scrape and thud of men scrambling down the steep earth bank and landing heavily on the road. Aitahang risked a look up over the lip of the ditch, and jerked his head down again at once. Chinese in light khaki uniforms were jumping down onto the road and running towards the trucks—a number towards the first truck, and half a dozen in his direction. There were urgent cries, curiously loud in the quiet after the firing, and he lay trying to restrain his unsteady breathing in case it gave him away. Slowly he dragged himself farther up the ditch and under the shelter of a canted-up wheel.

The running feet passed and he heard a familiar clink or two, interspersed with brief comments in Chinese, and knew they were picking up the rifles and ammunition of the dead soldiers. His heart beat in great thuds: if one of the terrorists thought of crawling under the truck to look in the ditch, he was finished. Then he heard just that happening. A gym shoe scraped, and he heard heavy breathing not three feet from his head. Then a Chinese voice said almost in his ear two syllables that Aitahang would remember for the rest of his life, '*Mo-yan*'. The terrorist had merely bent to look; the ditch had seemed empty; '*Mo-yan*,' he said, and got up again, dusting the knees of his trousers.

Aitahang felt his heart jump with relief, then sank again. The same Chinese voice called out from the truck above, and Aitahang knew that Manbahadur had been found alive.

A voice answered from along the road, an authoritative, harsh voice, and Aitahang heard the quick purposeful tread of feet striding up. He inched an eye over the lip of the ditch and caught a glimpse of thin legs in puttees and breeches come up and stop on the far side of the truck. There was a word or two, then to Aitahang's horror he heard the muffled crack of a pistol firing close into a body. The harsh voice spoke curtly, then the thin legs turned and strode away.

With a great effort Aitahang pushed himself up with his left arm and stared between the truck wheels at the thin legs marching off. As they strode on more and more of the man came into view—a khaki shirt, a narrow waist with a broad leather belt and heavy leather holster into which he was replacing an automatic pistol, a thin neck and bony head on which a peaked cloth cap was pulled on tight.

A Chinese by the truck called a query, the man with the pistol turned to reply and from the shadows under the truck Aitahang fixed a concentrated gaze on the face of the man who had commanded the ambush and who had murdered his friend. It was a face he would never forget, a thin, bony, cruel face, with prominent teeth capped with gold. But there was one unmistakable feature: that face had only one eye.

Slowly Aitahang let himself slip back down into the concealing ditch. Above him the Chinese in the truck were searching it thoroughly, throwing everything useful into a groundsheet spread out on the road—tools, the vehicle's first-aid kit, a map case taken from a dead N.C.O., even the vehicle's shovel. They were working hastily; several minutes had passed since the firing and they were anxious to scatter back into the concealing forest. Would they look again under the truck? Aitahang had little thought for that danger, he had only one thought in his mind; he would recover, and he would hunt down that one-eyed murderer if it were the last thing he ever did. There seemed a certainty in his mind about this, almost as if he had decided on it a long time ago, and this puzzled him; perhaps his mind was wandering a little with the effects of his wound. Blood was beginning to congeal beneath him, and he was terribly thirsty. But as he lay with his face against the earth of the ditch he heard a steady tremor. It continued for some moments, then there were warning cries and a rush of feet. Tools, the shovel, bandoleers of ammunition—all were abandoned and the terrorists scrambled for the high earth bank and above him he heard a snapping and crashing of bushes as men forced their way up through the undergrowth. The steady rumble grew louder and round the far corner swept an armoured car, its two pounder gun and Browning machine-gun traversing slowly.

At the sight of the ditched trucks and the dead Gurkhas it halted abruptly and slam-bang! slam-bang! the two-pounder opened fire into the hill-side above, followed at once by the tearing rattle of the Browning. There was a scraping noise and down the earth bank slid a khaki-clad body, slowly folding up in the ditch beyond him, and Aitahang caught a glimpse of a white face, staring unfocused eyes and long black hair. The Browning raked the hill-side but at length ceased fire. The rest had made good their escape.

There was the clang of a steel turret and the reassuring sound of leather boots on the road. An English voice called, 'Bad one, this—they're all dead!'

Aitahang tried to call out, but only managed a feeble cry. Boots ran towards his truck and a British soldier knelt to peer under it. 'Not all dead, sir,' he called. 'Here's one still alive.'

Aitahang gritted his teeth as they gently pulled him from under the truck, and only then did he relax and slip into unconsciousness.

He woke in the Regimental Aid Post at Battalion H.Q. He had been stripped of his bloodstained uniform, washed, and his right arm and chest were encased in plaster. He lay on a stretcher under a mosquito net, his head pillowed on blankets. There was a strong smell of ether, and as he turned his head a medical orderly got up from a chair and came over to him. 'You'll be off to the B.M.H. in Kuala Lumpur first thing in the morning,' he said. 'You were lucky—that bullet broke your shoulder-blade at the back and two ribs in front, but the Doctor Sahib says you'll be fighting fit again in a couple of months.'

Aitahang nodded. He felt weak and depressed.

'That was one of the worst ambushes we've had,' the medical orderly went on, 'only the two of you left alive.' He nodded at a motionless form on a stretcher across the room. 'He's badly shot—still unconscious. Two bullets in him, but he'll be all right.'

Aitahang turned his head feebly. 'Who is it?'

The orderly crossed the room and looked at the label tied to the wounded man. 'Sixty-six Twelve Manbahadur Limbu. Know him?'

'Yes,' answered Aitahang. He suddenly felt warm and sleepy. 'Yes, I know him.'

While Aitahang and Manbahadur travelled by ambulance to the military hospital in Kuala Lumpur, two companies of Gurkhas, hastily gathered in from other operations, were rushed to the scene of the ambush. Thirsting for revenge and spoiling for a fight they combed the forest behind the ambush spot, but as hours and then days passed they reported only failure. For some distance they were able to follow tracks, but these quickly separated, heading out in a dozen directions, and these faint traces were finally washed away in a storm of rain. The only clue was the terrorist killed by the armoured car's Browning machine-gun. He was carefully photographed and finger-printed by the Bentong police, and at last he was identified.

'We've got a surrendered C.T. who recognizes him,' announced the Police Superintendent to the Commanding Officer of the Battalion at their daily conference. 'He's one of the Chang mob, the so-called Seventh Company.'

'They don't operate round here,' objected the Colonel. 'Surely they've spent the past year up round Jerantut, much farther north!'

'They have,' agreed the Police Superintendent, 'but it looks as if they're beginning to take an interest in this area as well.'

'What do we know about Chang himself, the leader?'

'Quite a lot. He's been wanted for years. He started off as a gangster in the Singapore underworld, then after the war set about organizing strikes down in the Singapore docks—you remember, when they used to try and get some of the strikers to burn Europeans alive in their cars. Then he managed to slip across to Calcutta for the big Communist meeting there, when plans were laid to start revolution throughout South-East Asia. When he got back he dodged into the jungle across the Causeway, in Johore, and soon made himself commander of this gang there. He's rumoured to have had his predecessor killed in order to take over

—denounced him as a traitor and had him beaten to death with mattock handles. They do that when they want to save ammunition.'

'When did they leave Johore?'

'It's a year or two now—they set off with a dozen other gangs to try and take over a remote area of North Pahang and turn it into a real Communist area, you know, communes and such-like. But they were attacked on the way and split up, and since then have existed pretty much on their own. They're well armed—'

'I know, they've just got some of our weapons.' The Colonel spoke with ominous calm.

'Every man in that gang faces execution, for the things they've done. There's one important thing, though,' said the police officer with a hard smile, 'Chang is an easy man to recognize.'

'Why's that?'

'He wears a permanent reminder of a gang fight in Singapore. One of the opposition got him with a bicycle chain. He's only got one eye.'

'H'm.' The Colonel looked at the map thoughtfully. 'Any of your agents got ideas as to where this gang are hiding out?'

'No agent will go near them—too dangerous. They have nasty ways of punishing people they suspect to be traitors or police spies.' He frowned. 'Normally our people will take risks, for the rewards for information are good. But they won't take risks with this lot.'

'So we've absolutely no idea where they might be?'

'None whatever.' The Police Superintendent drew his hand slowly across the great map. 'They might be forty miles away—and they could just as easily be half a mile behind your own officers' mess.'

'So we must just keep patrolling.'

'Yes. And wait till they strike again.'

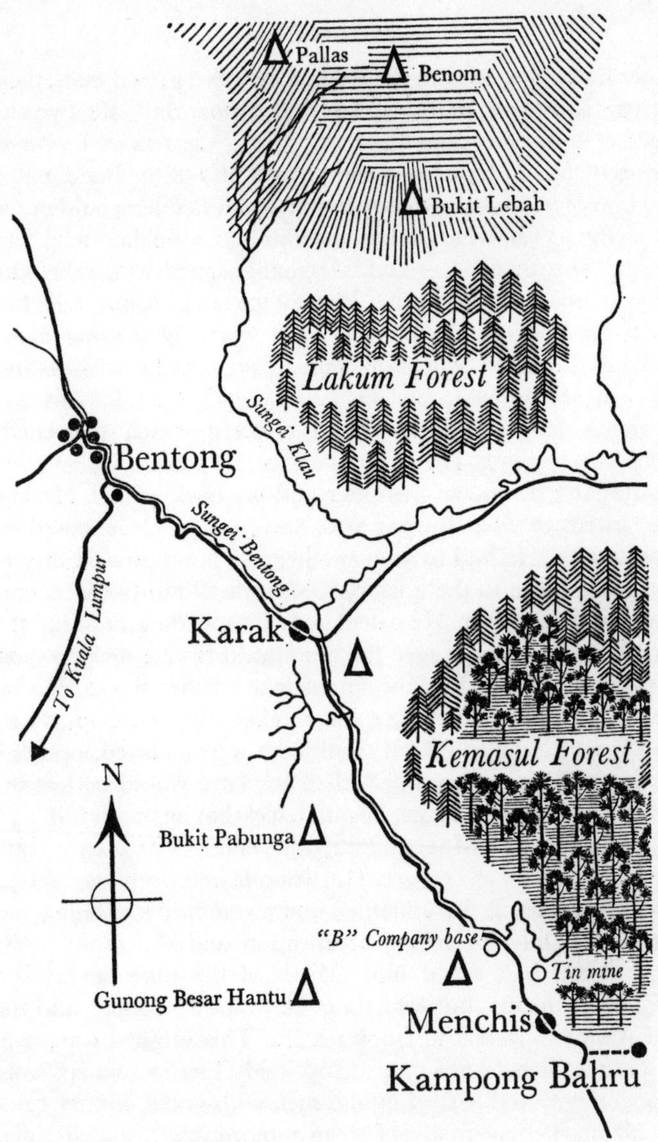


## 8 FIRST FIGHT

While he lay in hospital recovering from his wound Aitahang received a letter from his father, written on the coarse, fibrous hand-made paper of Nepal. He read the script slowly, for his father had only learnt to write when he was a grown man, picking it up here and there, and the result was clumsy, but effective enough. After opening greetings the letter said: 'We received your eighty rupees by hand of the leave man. I took fifty to the Phedangba, and told him of your desire to buy that land. At first he would not accept it, saying: "Of what use is the land to a soldier who may be killed?" But then he agreed.' Aitahang sighed with relief; he had never considered that the Phedangba might not sell to him. Then he read on, deciphering each word by reading aloud the individual letters. 'The Phedangba said that he was getting old. He will sell to you, but he cannot wait long for his money.' Aitahang felt a sudden stir of concern which deepened into anxiety as he read, 'He will wait a year, no more.'

Aitahang put down the letter and lay back in bed. He knew to the last rupee what his pay was, and how much he could put by each month. He had to save another five hundred and fifty rupees and get it home to the hills from Malaya within twelve months. It was now September. He calculated: by spending nothing at all of his pay he could just save the amount in twelve months—but the business of getting it home might take further weeks. He himself would not have home leave for another two years, so some leave men would have to take it; and if he were delayed, or fell ill on the journey, or were robbed, then the land would be lost to him. For the first time Aitahang began to feel that he might fail.

Beside him lay Manbahadur, also encased in plaster, but taking much longer to recover. His wounds had been very serious—a .303 rifle bullet in the abdomen and a 9 mm. pistol bullet through the chest. Only his strong constitution and the rapid arrival of medical aid had saved him. Much of the time he lay quietly, sleeping or dozing, but sometimes he would lie awake, and then he and Aitahang talked in Limbu Kura. This surgical ward was full of soldiers. It held not only British and Gurkha soldiers wounded in action with terrorists, but also men with grave injuries caused in vehicle accidents—many of them motor-cycle dispatch riders. So the quiet talk up and down the ward went on in half a dozen languages—Limbu Kura, Gurkhali, English, the Gurung and Magar Kuras of soldiers from West Nepal, and sometimes one or other of the numerous Rai languages. As one wounded Rai explained to Aitahang in Gurkhali, 'There are as many Kuras as Rais!'

But Aitahang's thoughts were now sombre. He asked the English ward sister for pen and paper, and wrote a lengthy letter to his father—his first since his wound—reassuring him about the injury, and asking that he see the Phedangba again and persuade him to extend the period; even another three months might make all the difference.

When he had written and asked that the letter be sent to Jalapahar for onward dispatch Aitahang lay pondering. The job of saving that money and getting it home to the Phedangba was quite enough for him to worry about for the time being. After all, it was his reason for running away from home to join the Army. Somewhat to his surprised irritation, however, into his thoughts of the land there kept obtruding a bony, one-eyed face under a red-starred peaked cloth cap, no matter how hard he tried to push that image away. During the long weeks in hospital his vow to hunt down the one-eyed terrorist had become rather remote, something undertaken at a time when his mind was unbalanced with stress and pain. On sober reflection it seemed an impossible quest: when half a battalion had failed to find the terrorists after the ambush, how could he—a young soldier of no experience—hope to hunt him down? He had better stick to getting his savings home. And yet . . . that one-eyed face stuck obstinately in his mind.

Aitahang eventually left hospital on his birthday, his eighteenth, according to Army records, but in fact his fifteenth. He spent two weeks' sick leave in a rest camp in Penang where he learnt to swim after a fashion, splashing about in the warm sea and acquiring a deep tan. This long stretch of sun and salt water did him the world of good, completing his cure, transforming his hospital pallor, and letting his muscles build up again. Then it was back to Bentong, interviews with the Adjutant and Gurkha Major and when the next ration convoys arrived, off again once more towards B Company.

This time his journey was uneventful, and they passed the hairpin bend without incident. It was curious, he pondered, as the convoy drove past the ditch where he had lain hidden, how he had felt that funny prickle at the back of his neck—rather like Bhalu's hairs ruffling up when he scented some wild animal. It had saved him, for if he had not leant forward to speak to the escort soldier that bullet would have struck him in the centre of the chest and killed him. But although the sight of the ambush spot did not tense his muscles with anticipation he felt it rekindle the fire of his hatred of One-Eye, and it flamed up again, fiercer than ever.

Somehow, he could not think how, he would catch up with One-Eye, and when he did he would kill him. He had changed since the ambush. Before it he had been a quiet Gurkha boy, accepting that the Army meant fighting, philosophically accepting the risk of wounds or death as part of the price of his pay. Now he felt a personal involvement; ambush was one thing, legitimate in war; but murder of the wounded put these terrorists outside the law. He had never imagined that he would look forward to facing men and killing with his own hand. Now he knew that he did.

Some dozen miles beyond the ambush spot they left the high hills behind them and entered a more open section, the hills standing back farther from the road, with areas of open paddy field cut out of the forest. They drove through these for a mile or two till they reached a point where a narrow track led off through dry paddy. It curved away into the hill-side and Aitahang could just see a portion of a vehicle canopy and a faint thread of smoke. The convoy turned along the track, bumped along it for two hundred yards and stopped at a small vehicle park cut into the hill-side. A thatched lean-to stood nearby, and a sparkling stream ran past. Behind this rose a small hill with a ridge running back into the forested hills. Aitahang was puzzled. 'Where's the company?' he asked, and one of the drivers laughed: 'Up on the hill. That's the idea—no one can tell whether the platoons are in base or out on operations.'

The duty N.C.O., the Line Orderly, was waiting down by the vehicle park, and he gave Aitahang his instructions, reminding him that he must always move armed. 'We haven't bumped any bandits here yet,' he said, 'but they're around all right, so be alert. Now, you'll be seen by the company second-in-command, Captain Lalsing. He's up the hill. Take your kit up with you.'

There was a steep climb up a zig-zag staircase cut against the hill-side and lined with slats of bamboo, but once up on top Aitahang looked round with delight. Instead of a formal military camp, he saw a group of rustic thatched huts and a few brown canvas tents, set here and there between enormous forest trees. The smaller trees had been felled, and sunshine filtered down through the high branches in a shifting leafy pattern. To one side biggish windows had been cut in the tree cover, and from this hill-top he could see out east and north, blue-green forest rolling away to the horizon, here and there interspersed with great peaks. Bamboo grew in profusion round the sides of this hill, adding its paler green to the darker forest leaves. The whole impression was of a dappled green shade, and the wooded hill-top position gave a feeling of security and concealment.

The hill-top huts were nearly empty, but he saw one or two soldiers resting on their blankets—relief sentries he guessed—and one of them showed him the small, thatched company office where a clerk sat at a six-foot G.S. table and a tall Gurkha captain at another. He saluted and reported his arrival.

'So-o,' the officer said slowly and deliberately, 'Sixty-Six Thirteen Rifleman Aitahang Limbu.' He nodded to himself as he read Aitahang's particulars, and changed from Gurkhali to the Limbu tongue. 'Mewa Khola, eh? Up beyond Changa?'

'Huzoor!' confirmed Aitahang, his heart warming at the sound of his mother tongue.

'Ever go across to Athrai?'

'Never that way, Huzoor—only travelled east of the Tambur.'

The Gurkha captain nodded without comment, but Aitahang now knew where he came from—the great Athrai glen, remote and high, west of the River Tambur. While he spoke the officer carefully bound a tiny split in the handle of his kukri with fine wire, seeming to pay Aitahang little attention, then after a pause he said, 'So you were wounded in that ambush up between Kuala Padah and Karak. How are you now, fit for patrolling?'

'Fit, Huzoor.'

The officer nodded. 'Very good. Everyone's out now with the Major Sahib, but on their return you will join Four Platoon. If you have any trouble or queries, you know how they are dealt with?'

'Yes, Huzoor—I ask to see you through my platoon commander.'

'That is right. I see to all religious and family matters, but if it is official, that is, military, it will be looked into by the company commander Sahib.' He fell to studying the handle of his kukri again, looked up and said, 'Go down to the cookhouse now and get something to eat,' and nodded dismissal.

Aitahang saluted, hurried out, quickly opened his pack and took out mess-tin, mug and spoon, and hurried down the zig-zag steps.

The chubby cook was another Limbu. He quizzed Aitahang as he heaped his plate with rice, spices and hot split peas. 'D'ye eat meat? You a meat-eater?' He gave a fat chuckle. 'We've a good number of vegetarians in this company,' he whispered when he found Aitahang was a Limbu, 'most of them these Rais from Bhojpur. All the more for the rest of us!' As he gave Aitahang meat he asked in Limbu Kura where he came from, and when he heard Mewa Khola, made a wry face: 'You've walked a mile or two in your time, sonny!' He looked at Aitahang again, more closely. 'How'd you manage, boy—you're a bit young aren't you?' Then he gave a conspiratorial wink. 'Never mind—it's been done before!'

Aitahang breathed a sigh of relief. He was still secretly conscious of the enormous disparity between his official and actual ages.

The company returned to base that evening, filtering in from the ridge behind and gathering in platoon groups on the beaten-earth open space in the centre of the hill-top. As the three platoon commanders reported to the company commander for dismissal Aitahang, watching from the trees, studied him curiously. He saw a man slightly above average height, thin with much walking, pale-faced through lack of sun, with a light brown moustache, light brown hair and the pale eyes of Europeans. His webbing equipment was worn and rather frayed. In a holster on his left hip he wore a big automatic pistol of a kind Aitahang had not seen before, and a good kukri on his right side. He was quite old, Aitahang noted, at least thirty. Aitahang was rather disappointed at first, for there seemed nothing special about him; he looked more or less like all the other British officers he had seen. Perhaps, he guessed with a flash of insight, that was the secret strength of these British—they were all rather like each other.

When the company was dismissed Aitahang waited shyly at the Four Platoon huts till he was sent for by the platoon commander. He at once asked after Aitahang's wound and shook his head as he talked of the ambush. 'A bad one, lad—and a big gang, too. Nobody seems to know where they hide out—they seemed to have sprung up from nowhere! But we'll get them sooner or later!' He looked at Aitahang appraisingly. 'So you're from Mewa Khola, eh? That's far up! Shepherd?'

'Shepherd, Huzoor.'

'Very good. Now, you will join One Section; that's Corporal Bhimbahadur. Report to him straight away and he'll fix you up with a sleeping place and tell you your duties.'

'Huzoor!'

'You know to come to me through your section commander if you have any problems?'

'I know, Huzoor.'

'Good. Don't forget, now.' He gave him a friendly nod and walked off, a small, rather wizened man with fierce keen eyes.

'What's the platoon commander's name?' whispered Aitahang to one of the soldiers busy nearby cleaning his rifle.

'He's Lieutenant Narsing Limbu, from Tehra Thum.'

The N.C.O. in charge of One Section was Corporal Bhimbahadur Limbu, a round-faced soldier from the south of Limbuan, down near Panchhthar. He spoke to Aitahang in a grave tone, and carefully noted his particulars in his section book, which he produced from a waterproof oilskin wallet. From the first he addressed Aitahang in regimental fashion, by his last two numbers. 'You will be armed with a rifle, Thirteen,' he said when he had completed his note-taking, 'and you will be in a rifle group with Lalbir Tamang and Jagatman Rai. The other group is the bren group.' He put his notebook carefully away. 'You'll come with us tomorrow—we'll probably be on day patrol.'

While the company settled down to sleep when darkness fell the company commander, the second-in-command and the three platoon commanders met to discuss operations. After the Major had poured out a tot of rum for each they pulled round their map-cases, opened the webbing covers and studied the expanse of contoured greens and browns. So far B Company had achieved little success: the enemy had remained elusive and quiet, so much so that back in Battalion H.Q. it was suspected that when the Gurkha company had moved in and built its camp there three months before, the terrorists had moved away. But the Major thought otherwise.

'Once again we've found nothing,' he said, frowning at the map, 'not a new footprint, only one or two abandoned camps months old.'

The Gurkha officers drank their rum in silence.

'It is said that the gang who used to ambush down here have moved out.' He shook his head. 'I don't believe it. They're here somewhere—but unless we get proof very soon we'll be moved to another area, and then the ambushes and murders down here will start all over again.'

'D Company are very busy up around Kuala Padah and Karak,' said the second-in-command in his slow drawl, 'we might get some more action up there, helping them look for that gang that ambushed the convoy.'

'They'll be miles away,' objected the Major. 'They wouldn't have done a big ambush close to their own base. No,' he shook his head, 'that lot are far away from there.'

'Maybe even down here, Sahib,' suggested Four Platoon commander.

'Maybe.' The Major looked doubtful. 'It doesn't *feel* like it, somehow. I just can't smell that lot around. But there's something here, I know.'

The others nodded. They all knew the feeling when terrorists had settled in a forest area; there seemed to be something in the air that old hands at forest warfare could detect. 'Yes, there's something here.' The Major passed the rum bottle around. 'There must be the usual Min Yuen plain-clothes mob near the villages and the uniformed gang deeper in the forest.' He drank up his rum. 'We'll try again with small section patrols, starting tomorrow.'

The next morning the platoon commanders gave orders to their section commanders and Corporal Bhimbahadur returned and spread out his map to give his section their orders, and Aitahang was able to see the extent of B Company's area. It was bounded on the north by a small river, a few miles north of the base, and on the south by the State boundary with Negri Sembilan—no more than a dotted line on the map. But east and west boundaries did not exist. On one side lay the peaks between this area and the plains of Kuala Lumpur, on the other, many days' march away, the swamps south of the Pahang river. Through this huge area ran the one narrow winding road, a village or two, and, not far south of the B Company base but a mile or so into the forest, a tin mine. Everything else was forested mountain, plain or swamp.

'We are going on a day patrol,' explained Bhimbahadur, 'to check on the jungle area just behind the village of Manchis. The other sections will be off in other directions, and Five and Six Platoons are to patrol across the road, around the tin mine.'

They ate before leaving and the section commander inspected the men and their equipment. 'Usual formation,' he said, 'leading scout, then me, then bren group and rifle group. We'll change the leading scout every half-hour, as usual, and if we find bandits, rush 'em—again as usual.' He paused a moment. 'Any questions?'

'Any police patrols about?' asked the bren-gunner.

'None. Anything we meet is enemy. Right, then—load!'

Aitahang loaded his rifle with impassive face, but inside him he began to feel a heightened tension. Once beyond the sentry post they might find themselves engaged in close-range fighting at any moment. He was annoyed with himself for his excitement—he must calm down if he were to fight efficiently.

'Coming, Thirteen?' He started. The others were quietly beginning to move off. He clicked his tongue with embarrassment and followed, annoyed with himself for dreaming, yet content.

They left the company base by the back way, the forest ridge. Once past the camouflaged sentry-post they separated, keeping several yards between each man. Somewhat to Aitahang's surprise their pace was slow, almost casual; the leading scout went quietly along with his rifle tucked under his arm, occasionally looking back to the section commander for direction. Tense and eager, Aitahang clutched his rifle tightly, ready to fling it up and open fire at a moment's notice. He began to feel irritated; this section were being rather lackadaisical about the important business of killing terrorists; they should get a move on, and hasten to the fight! Then as the minutes dragged past he began to realize that there was nowhere to hurry to; in this vast forest the enemy might be behind the next tree—or over the next mountain. Haste would only mean noise, and in this forest the quiet man won.

All the time his eyes were busy looking right and left for signs on the ground—he hardly realized he was doing this, so much had observation become part of him—and he noted that apart from one or two prints left weeks ago by Gurkhas themselves (their diamond-soled pattern unmistakable) there was little of interest. 'Tss-ss!' The section commander hissed, everyone froze, he gestured and the leading scout was replaced by the rifleman at the rear. They all stood listening for a moment, then he waved the scout on again. Another half-hour passed, he hissed again and gestured and they all sank down, resting in silence. In ten minutes he waved them up, the scout changed again, and on they went between the trees.

Aitahang was used to lonely uninhabited areas, but this unbroken gloom, the countless trees, the spaces between them filled with curving fronds of all shapes and sizes, many with a double line of hook-like thorns running down their spines, gradually made him understand why finding and killing even one terrorist was a considerable feat. Perhaps, he thought, his experience of tracking might come in useful, but he felt diffident about mentioning it; these men had been hunting bandits for many months, and it was his job to learn.

One thing he would have to learn quickly, though, were the names of the others in the section. Mentally he went through them. There was the section commander, Bhimbahadur; then the rifle group commander, a moody-looking Rai called Jagatman, and with him in the rifle group a Tamang called Lalbir. The commander of the bren group was a Lance-Corporal, a Sunwar from above the Sun Kosi called Bombahadur; his bren-gunner was another Limbu, Kulbahadur—Aitahang remembered him easily because of two handsome gold teeth in the front of his mouth—and the gunner's number two was Kesersing Rai. He must remember all these, and quickly learn their regimental numbers.

So they progressed all morning—moving slowly through the trees, at intervals sitting down to rest and listen, then moving on again. At one o'clock they had a whole hour off, sitting spread out and silent while one man made tea on a small fire of sticks. To his surprise Aitahang found that he was quite tired; this patrolling business, apparently easy enough, was in fact hard work.

By three o'clock in the afternoon they had come in a great half circle and had reach the forest fringe behind the rice fields of Manchis. These stuck out into the forest like long fingers from the village itself, a good mile away by the road. The rice fields were dry and uncultivated, fringed with belukar and edged with encroaching trees.

All day Aitahang had walked quietly in the section with the knowledge that in the stretch of forest they moved in there were no other men—animals enough, but no men. As the seven Gurkhas crouched at the forest edge, however, he suddenly felt that there were other men close to them. He saw nothing, he could smell nothing, yet he knew; the back of his neck prickled. He gestured to Bombahadur who raised an eyebrow and Aitahang rather hesitantly nodded down towards the uneven little strip of paddy field near which they had paused. Bombahadur also had a very tense expression on his face, and he caught Bhimbahadur's eye. The section commander gave a hand signal and the section split into its two little groups, and spread out, Bombahadur and his rifle group to the left, the section commander and his bren group to the right, then both groups began working their way carefully through the belukar.

At length they came on to the edge of the little clearing. In front of them stretched the long fingers of open paddy fields, and behind them the tall forest. Nowhere was there a sign of men. Aitahang felt both irritated with himself and rather puzzled. The feeling of men was stronger than ever, yet the clearing just below them was quite empty. He looked across the few yards to the bren group, standing in knee-high grass; the bren-gunner had put down his heavy weapon by the butt, obviously not expecting to have to use it. Aitahang turned to Bombahadur, noticing that he still looked worried, but said to him apologetically, 'There's no one here that I can see.'

As he spoke he knew he was wrong. The old cultivation started a few yards in front of them—and three or four feet below. What had appeared to be waist-high lalling grass in front was shorter, and grew over a hidden bank, and from beneath this bank he heard a rustle, abruptly stilled. He put his hand over his lips and jerked his head. Bombahadur and Jagatman had heard it too. Then from the concealing shelter of the bank sprang two men in tattered blue jackets and trousers. One dashed straight across for the shelter of the trees on the far side of the clearing, the other turned, swung up a shot-gun and fired. Aitahang felt the sting of a weapon being fired directly at him, and heard the swish of grass beside his thigh as something heavy whistled past him. He fired his rifle at once, missed, and desperately reloaded, but beside him Jagatman said casually, 'I'll get him,' slid up his rifle and fired once, then without waiting to watch the man stagger and fall, aimed again and fired at the second man—now only a yard or two from the shelter of the trees. He fell backwards onto the cracked earth, and silence fell again over the clearing and the forest.

Aitahang stared across at the two men. One, who had fired at him, was still breathing, for his chest heaved up and down, and Aitahang moved forward, anxious to seize that shot-gun in case he struggled up and fired again. But 'Wait!' commanded Bombahadur, holding up a hand in warning. He moved a few yards farther to the left, then with a great leap sprang out into the clearing and fired his rifle into the still invisible shelter of the bank. From above Aitahang heard the light crack of a pistol. Bombahadur fired again, then lowered his rifle. Warily looking at something the others could not see he said briefly—'That's the lot.'

'Quick—across to the far side!' They plunged down and ran across and up into the tangle of short jungle beyond. 'See any more?' panted the section commander. 'Sweep the area!'

Out here in the open it was intensely hot. Partially shut in by the trees there was not a breath of air stirring in the old paddy fields, and the sun blazed down, making the sweat burst out from them as they ran. Aitahang's heart was pounding with exertion and excitement; he could still hear the swish of the heavy projectile through the grass beside him. It had been a bit too close. He was consumed with thirst, but as they hurried around the tangled edges, looking for more of the enemy, his main worry was the knowledge that he had fired at a terrorist at close range and had missed him completely.

Suddenly there was a cry of warning and rifles swung up as a soldier broke back from the jungle edge and staggered into the paddy fields. 'What on earth—'

'Hornets!' he cried out, his face muffled and a swarming cloud of vicious insects about his head. 'A hornets' nest!' The Gurkhas scattered away, and only after several minutes of beating and flailing did they reassemble, all stung more or less badly, faces and necks swollen and painful.

'Let's get out of here,' said Bhimbahadur thickly, mopping his face. 'Tie 'em up.'

Aitahang now saw how successful patrol actions ended. Two soldiers went up into the short belukar fringe, there was the sound of kukris chopping, and they returned in a few minutes with three ten-foot poles and long lengths of creeper.

'Stretch 'em out.' The three dead terrorists were dragged out till they lay more or less straight. 'That's it. Now cross their legs over the poles and tie 'em on, like this,' and Kulbahadur the bren-gunner showed Aitahang how the lashings were made round the men's ankles. 'Next, tie their arms round the poles, tight as you can.'

They poured with sweat as they worked at their unpleasant task. 'Now wrap lots of creeper right round them, so that they're tight against the pole—they're awkward to carry if they dangle too much.'

Aitahang began to feel rather unsteady. He could hardly swallow with thirst, flies were beginning to buzz about them, he had received half a dozen painful hornet stings and the relief that had flooded over him when the fight ended was beginning to ebb away.

'Next, sling on their weapons,' grunted Kulbahadur. 'Here's this man's shot-gun. Just check that it's empty.' He broke it open. 'That's all right.' He extracted the empty cartridge case, then looked in the dead man's haversack. It was full of cartridges. He pulled one out, examined it and whistled. 'Lucky he didn't get you with one of those,' he said in a dry tone. 'See what he's done to it?'

Aitahang wiped the sweat from his eyes with his sleeve and looked at the red cartridge. 'I can't see any difference,' he confessed, 'I don't know much about these.'

'He's taken out the top bit of cardboard and poured in melted candle wax. Then he's made two slits with a razor blade just above the end of the charge.'

'What does that do?'

'When he fires, the shot comes out all together in a huge slug of lead, bigger than your thumb. A wound anywhere from one of these and you're finished. If it hit you square on, of course, it'd cut you nearly in half.'

Aitahang mopped his face again, in silence. If it had not been for the steady shooting of the others he too would be lying dead and his comrades would carry him back slung on a pole. There and then he made his third great resolve: he would learn to be the killer, not the killed.

'All ready?' called Bhimbahadur. 'Right, then, up with 'em.'

Two by two the Gurkhas lifted the poles.

'Why do we have to carry them in?' Aitahang asked Kulbahadur as he settled the weighty pole on his shoulder.

'Get 'em identified. Also shows we really killed 'em.'

'Let's go, lads,' called Bhimbahadur and they set off with their swaying, bumping burdens towards the distant road.

# 9 THE ELEPHANT

Alerted by reports of firing west of Manchis, the Major met the section at the point in the road where they had dumped the three bodies. He examined them with a practised eye: 'Min Yuen, all right—coolie clothing, pistols and a shot-gun, typical weapons.' He looked at the soldiers standing impassively, then spotted Aitahang. 'You've brought us luck, Thirteen.' Aitahang said nothing. It hadn't really been luck; he had sensed their presence, but they would all have got away had it not been for the shooting of Jagatman, and Bombahadur's discovery of the third man.

'We'll drop these characters in at the police post—they'll do the necessary finger-printing and photographing. Up with them into the truck!'

The Malay police, who had telephoned news of the noise of shooting to B Company H.Q., were even more pleased to see the dead Min Yuen than the Major. Living as they did in sandbagged isolation outside a Chinese-inhabited village, exposed to attack from any direction, this diminution in the number of their enemies was welcome, and they opened bottles of beer for the soldiers and the Malay police officer in charge produced tins of cigarettes. Once back at base, however, the Major wasted no time in summoning his platoon commanders.

'All patrols in now, and only one contact—here!' and he laid his pencil point on the map just west of the village. 'Now, what does that suggest to you, Captain Sahib?' and he nodded towards the company second-in-command.

'These Min Yuen don't exist in isolation, therefore there is a uniformed gang about somewhere.'

'Yes. Now what about the place where they were found?'

'It was west of the village. They were probably waiting till dark to enter the village.'

'I agree. But what about the direction, Sahib—what does it suggest to you?' and the Major nodded to Four Platoon commander.

'Of course! They would not approach the village from the direction of the gang's hideout!'

'Exactly. Whatever else we know or don't know, we can be sure of one thing—the direction of their approach is *not* the direction of their camp. Now then, let's do a bit of thinking.' The officers sat studying their maps, eyes translating the contours, colours and wiggly river lines into a picture of just what each stretch of country was like—how accessible, how steep, and whether swamp escape-routes existed behind dry ground; above all, whether or not it was within reasonable supply distance from some village or other source of food.

While the officers were discussing the next moves, One Section were down at the cookhouse. 'Eat up!' commanded the chubby cook Harkadhan as he heaped their mess-tins with rice and meat. 'You can't fight on an empty stomach.' His eyes twinkled as he filled Aitahang's mess-tin. 'You look weary, son—it's hard work, fighting!'

Aitahang forced a smile in return, but in reality he was deeply depressed. The long hours of careful movement, the brief fury of the fight, the long haul over baking-hot paddy fields burdened with a dead man on a pole, all had left him exhausted. But on top of this was the knowledge that when faced with an enemy he had been quite unable to kill him, and had himself only survived through the good shooting of another soldier. The hot food cheered him somewhat, and back up at the section hut, he spoke diffidently to Jagatman, lying on his blankets smoking a cigarette. 'I missed that first one,' he said awkwardly, 'that shot-gun fellow.'

Jagatman glanced up at him without comment.

'You shot him,' went on Aitahang doggedly, 'then you shot the next one.'

The other soldier blew out a cloud of smoke and said casually, 'You mean, why did you miss? And if *you* missed, how did *I* manage to get them?'

Rather embarrassed Aitahang said, 'Yes, that's it. I aimed all right, but I still missed.'

Jagatman gave a humourless smile. 'You probably weren't looking.'

Startled, Aitahang said, 'But I was aiming right at him!' But Jagatman interrupted him, 'I'll tell you,' and Aitahang fell silent.

'If you want to succeed in a fight,' said Jagatman, 'you must put out of your mind what the enemy may do to you. Instead, you must concentrate on what you are going to do to *him*. Now, you started off meaning to shoot that first man, and you lifted your rifle and took aim. The trouble is, when you're aiming at one man you cannot see what anyone else is up to, especially with these new rifles with ring sights. You suspect that perhaps some other bandit is aiming at *you*. So, although you start by aiming at your man, by the time you press the trigger your eyes are wandering somewhere else.'

'I understand,' said Aitahang thoughtfully. 'I fired blind.'

'You fired blind. You must pick your man and you must think only of him. If you get him, that's one less to worry about and'—he gave a hard smile—'it worries the others and puts *them* off. In a fight take it steady, and take one man at a time. That way you'll live.' Jagatman stubbed out his cigarette, put it away tidily in the section waste-box and began to let down his mosquito net on its bamboo frame. Aitahang took the hint: it was time for sleep. He unloosed his net, tucked it in around the blankets, climbed in and stretched out. He settled himself to think back over each moment of the fight, so that he could identify the point at which he had wandered from his aim, but the moment his muscles relaxed on the bamboo mat he fell into a heavy sleep.

In the company commander's little hut the discussion on the whereabouts of the terrorist hideout continued. 'We've agreed that it won't be west of the village,' said the Major. 'Now that we've had a good look at the map let's think about other directions. What about north?

'Won't be north, Sahib—we ourselves are sitting three miles north of the village,' said the second-in-command.

'Agreed. North is also out. South?'

One officer commented, 'There are two big Malay kampongs down in that direction towards the Negri border. I think the Chinese terrorists would prefer not to be too near the Malays.'

'I think you are right. That leaves only one direction.'

'East, Sahib.'

'Yes, east beyond the mine.' He pondered a moment or two, then went on, 'We'll have a day off tomorrow, then we'll take the whole company in, entering from the Malay area down in the south and swinging up and around behind the mine. Once we're east of it we'll spread out in three directions by platoons, patrol till we find tracks, then close in when we find where they lead.'

'Four days' rations, Sahib?'

'Yes. If we've found nothing by that time we'll have to look somewhere else.'

The day's rest did them all good. It was spent in quiet preparations: torn clothing was mended or exchanged, ammunition inspected and checked, new primers put in grenades—for these spoilt quickly in the damp Malayan climate—and blankets dried in the open space down by the cookhouse. Also, the Gurkhas had a day without wearing sweat-soaked uniforms and heavy bandoleers of ammunition, a day to relax, and one or two small parties set off to hunt wild boar.

Aitahang was now beginning to know the others in his section rather better. At first just names and faces, they were taking on their own distinctive personalities. Corporal Bhimbahadur the section commander, who had fought in that same battalion in the Burma campaign at the age of 16, he found a very serious, quiet man. Next was the section second-in-command, Lance-Corporal Bombahadur Sunwar, slight of build and wearing the Oriental sign of good fortune, half a dozen smallpox scars. Aitahang remembered that he too had in some way sensed the presence of the Min Yuen—and also the third man hidden under the bank.

But Jagatman was Aitahang's hero. Moody and rather unapproachable he seldom joined in the section chat, instead lying on his blankets, smoking and listening. He was a Rai from Bhojpur, and Aitahang remembered his father's comment: 'Rais have hot tempers.' In B Company there seemed almost as many Rais as Limbus. Jagatman too had fought in the war as a young soldier, first in Burma against the Japanese and later in Java, against the Indonesians. Aitahang thought back to the effortless killing of the two Min Yuen, and wondered what memories of bloody fights lay behind that expressionless face.

Kulbahadur the bren-gunner had a mouthful of gold teeth of which he was very proud. 'Whenever we go down to Johore Bahru on our rest and retraining periods I get a couple done,' he explained. 'There's a Chinese dentist there, in Jalan Ibrahim, who does a wonderful job. I'll take you when we next go down, if you like.'

'But it must be expensive,' Aitahang expostulated. For him gold had only one purpose—to buy land. Putting it in one's mouth seemed a terrible waste. But Kulbahadur laughed, his eyes disappearing into slits. 'It looks good,' he said, 'and you can always have it taken out!' Aitahang shook his head politely. Kulbahadur was a good-hearted chap, but he was wrong about using gold for his teeth. He was rather excitable for a Limbu, Aitahang decided—but he had heard that Kulbahadur had already killed two Chinese terrorists in other areas, which meant that he was cool enough in action.

The last two members of the section were Kesersing Rai and Lalbir Tamang. Kesersing was taller than most Gurkhas, and had a more pronounced bone formation of the head and face. His eyes were set wide apart and turned upwards at the corners. He had a slightly more prominent nose and all this, together with his skin, more golden than the wheat-coloured complexions of the hill Gurkhas, reminded Aitahang of the look of the Bhotiyas in their robes and felt boots occasionally met with on the high ground above the Gurkha farms. Kesersing's home village was one of the clusters of stone and log houses on the west side of the Kangchenjunga range, usually snowed in during the winter with their goats and their half-yak cattle. Possibly he was of mixed descent, his father a Rai far from home, his mother a Sherpani, or even a Tibetan woman.

Lalbir Tamang was quite a normal hillman. He came from a well-known Tamang village above the Rawa Khola, far to the west of Limbuan. Short, lean and smiling, he was a Buddhist, and as such was able to eat beef, forbidden to the Hindu Gurkhas, and occasionally the company commander gave him a tin of bully beef from his own rations, when he sat and ate apart.

This rest-day gave Aitahang an opportunity to unwrap and inspect his Limbu kukri. When he unwound the cloth he drew the blade with a touch of anxiety, for he had seen too often what the ever-present damp of Malaya did to steel. He breathed with relief when he saw that the blade was still flawless, and he wiped it thoroughly and applied a fresh coating of thin oil.

Before he slid it back into its scabbard Bombahadur Sunwar asked to look at it. 'That's a real weapon you have there,' he murmured. He held the blade up, turned it this way and that, studied the edge and examined the buffalo-horn handle. 'This gives me strange thoughts,' he went on, talking carefully. 'This won't have been used?'

Aitahang understood. 'No, this kukri has not yet—worked.'

'H'm.' Still holding it, Bombahadur said, 'You do not take it on operations?'

'No, Huzoor—what is the use? My issue kukri does well enough; I'd only spoil this one taking it out on patrol.'

'Of course.' Bombahadur handed it back, but again he said, 'And are you sure you will never take it?'

'Quite sure. It is too good to use in rough jungle work, chopping wood and slashing down branches and so on. No,' and Aitahang shook his head firmly, rather surprised at Bombahadur's curious persistence, 'I will keep it here in my kitbag, carefully wrapped up.'

Near the end of the morning there was the sudden bang of a rifle shot close by, and Aitahang dropped the equipment he was cleaning and sprang for his rifle, but there was a call from someone on the hill-top—'That'll be a *shikar* party, probably got something—' and sure enough there soon came a shout for a carrying party. Half a dozen Gurkhas ran down the hill with their rifles, shirts flapping, and Aitahang followed. Three hundred yards into a fold of the hill beyond the cookhouse they came to one of the hunters, who called, 'We got a big boar!' and a short distance on they came to the second hunter, sitting beside a big brownish-grey hump on the ground. Energetically the Gurkhas set about cutting a strong pole and lashing the boar to it by its feet with lashings of flexible vine—rather as the section had served the Min Yuen the day before, thought Aitahang with a grimace.

He kept glancing at the carcass as he worked. Never before had he seen a Malayan boar at close quarters, and he was impressed by its size. It was enormously heavy, and covered with stiff bristles. It had narrow flanks and small hindquarters, a deep chest and a massive head and jaws, from which stuck out two pairs of short tusks. He ran a finger along one of them; through rubbing up and down against each other these tusks had developed rear edges like razors. A slash from one of these would cut a man open.

'Any trouble with this one?' he asked the soldier who had shot it.

'Not much; he came at us, but the first round knocked him over.' The man spoke casually, but Aitahang knew that if he had missed the pole might not have been for the boar. Here was another who had not faltered with his aim. The lesson was being driven home: one steady shot was worth any number badly aimed.

'Right, lads—off to the cookhouse!'

Harkadhan was waiting, his knives sharp and his fire blazing, and two helpers were ready with their kukris. In a few minutes the animal was cleaned, skinned and jointed, and the lean meat was being chopped up on a board by the two kukris. It was then put on to a slow boil, and by evening B Company were eating curried lean pork with their rice and vegetables. It was a good end to the day.

The next morning they were up in darkness and into their trucks, and by dawn were dismounting at the groves of fruit trees and the terraced fields of the Malay smallholders, south-east of Manchis, and surprised Malay Home Guards armed with single-barrelled shot-guns greeted them warmly. '*Selamat Pagi*,' they called. 'Good morning!' and the Gurkhas waved as they swung on their packs and set out for the forest edge.

Where the smallholdings ended and the forest trees began, however, the Gurkhas looked with surprise at two or three of the Malay houses which leant over at drunken angles, roofs half-shedding their thatch and the wooden beams thrust aside. The Gurkhas asked in Bazaar Malay what had happened, and a villager in a short sarong called back: '*Gajah!*' and waved around at more destruction—fruit trees stripped, leaves scattered about and branches and the husks of fruit littering the ground.

'Elephants!' muttered the Gurkhas, and looked warily at the broad footprints and the enormous footballs of wet grassy dung. 'It's that Durian fruit,' explained Bombahadur as they trudged on past the destruction. 'The elephants go wild for it when it's ripe. But they don't often come breaking into the kampongs for it.' He frowned. 'There must be a bad one in charge of this herd. We see these Malayan elephants often enough in the forest, and usually they're placid enough—but sometimes you get a real villain.'

Aitahang took one look at the nearest footprint and said, 'He was here early this morning.' He glanced at other footprints as they walked along. 'And there were two—no, three elephants here; I think, one big male and two cows, and—yes, there was a fourth, half-grown only, a half-grown calf.' One or two of the others in the section looked round in surprise. They, too, had been hill shepherds and farmers before enlisting, but knew they could not have rattled off this information with such rapid confidence. Jagatman drawled, 'And what were they called, sonny—Singe, Dharke and Pangray?'—common pet names for cattle in Nepal. Aitahang grinned; he realized that he must have sounded a little pompous, and he mumbled sheepishly, 'Don't know, Huzoor.'

He mused a moment or two as he walked along, smiling at a memory of himself as a small boy in Taplejung, listening to some ancient tale about Rajah Jangbahadur and an elephant. That was the day he remembered more for the gift of his first kukri.

By the time the sun was well up and the morning mist steaming away the Gurkhas were clear of the Malay smallholdings and into the forest. The platoon commanders were given final orders by the Major, and the soldiers seized the chance to sit and rest, and Aitahang sat on the ground and leaned against his pack.

He was glad to get its weight off his shoulders, even for a moment or two; each little respite counted for something when a long day's march through forest lay ahead—and the pack was heavy. It contained four days' rations of rice, tinned fish and biscuits and his share of the platoon's sugar; a tin of condensed milk and some tea. He also had a pair of gym shoes and a complete dry uniform to sleep in; a mosquito net which he shared with two other men—who each carried a lightweight blanket—and a broad waterproof poncho cape for roofing the night shelter. In his pouches he had a grenade and two of the dozen filled bren-gun magazines distributed throughout the section; round his chest was slung a cloth bandoleer holding fifty rounds of .303 ammunition; on his belt hung his issue kukri and in the crook of his arm he carried his rifle, loaded and charged with ten rounds.

'*Kambar Kas!*' The order to buckle belts was whispered from man to man. They pushed themselves up and checked their equipment.

'*Hin!*' came the order to set off, and the platoons moved off quietly through the trees on their separate ways.

All morning Four Platoon walked north through the forest towards the hills behind the tin mine. Just after midday, however, there came a warning mutter from the leading section: 'Elephants!'

'Where?'

'Over on the right.'

Lieutenant Narsing Limbu ordered quietly, 'Bren-gunners, stay ready!' and the Gurkhas unslung their weapons. 'Keep going steadily,' he commanded. 'Take it calmly and maybe they'll leave us alone.'

Aitahang could just make out the grey shapes—first one, then a second and third, with a fourth and much smaller one close behind. Almost at once three turned and melted away between the trees with astonishing speed and silence, but the largest remained, moving along in uneasy fashion, no more than forty yards away.

'That's the bull,' whispered Lalbir to Aitahang. 'Look at those tusks!'

The Gurkhas increased their pace through the trees. They did not worry overmuch, for they knew that they could kill the big beast with their brens if he charged, but the noise would warn every Chinese terrorist for miles around. However, the bull elephant made no attempt to charge, contenting himself with moving along with the platoon, sometimes on one side, sometimes on the other, until as the afternoon began to weaken into evening he disappeared. 'Just as well,' grunted the section commander, 'we'll have to make camp pretty soon—we must be just at the edge of the patrol area, and night is coming on.'

This was Aitahang's first night bivouac on a forest operation, and he made careful note of the busy, silent activity that began when the platoon commander noted a suitable stream and ordered, 'Make camp!'

The very first action of all was for the three sections each to send out a two-man patrol, to make sure that enemy were not close by.

'That happened to us once, in the early days,' said Bombahadur with a grimace. 'We marched too long and had to make camp in darkness, without patrolling first. In the morning we found that we had been sleeping about twenty yards from a big force of bandits that we'd been trying to find for months.'

'What happened?' asked Aitahang eagerly. 'Was there a big battle?'

'Nothing of the sort. They heard us make camp, packed up very quietly and moved off. That was up in the Gunong Benom foothills about a year ago. No one has seen that gang since—at least, not when they wanted to.'

While the patrols were out no time was wasted by the others. The platoon signaller made wireless contact with Company H.Q., now some three thousand yards away, saplings were cut for the shelters—not with kukris, for the noise of chopping carried far, but silently, with little saws—these saplings were thrust into the ground and poncho capes tied out tight with a double slope like a little roof, and bundles of leaves gathered and laid down as mattresses. While this went on small fires were lit and the rice put on, and when the patrols returned in half an hour to report all clear the night camp was ready. In another ten minutes everyone had downed a hot meal, swallowed a tot of rum and was preparing for sleep. Double night sentries sat in the ring of shelters, the cicadas burst into their evening song, and when the last of the light faded all but the sentries were deep in the sleep of fatigue.

It rained hard during the night, and the next day dawned heavy and overcast. Everything was damp, and the soldiers shivered as they changed out of their dry sleeping uniforms into their day clothing, impregnated with wood-smoke where it had been roughly dried by the evening's cooking fires.

'One Section will patrol west and south, Two Section west and Three Section west and north,' ordered Lieutenant Narsing.

The sections left their bivouacs intact, in case they found nothing and slept again in that spot. Armed only with weapons and ammunition they set out as soon as they had eaten their morning rice.

With Lalbir Tamang as leading scout and Aitahang his number two the section set off. For some little while they progressed quietly through the trees, then Aitahang whistled softly and the leading scout stopped and looked back. Aitahang made the sign for a footprint and Corporal Bhimbahadur behind him came up. 'What do you see, Thirteen?'

Aitahang pointed. 'Two men walked here yesterday.'

'You sure? I can't see very much there.'

'Most of it's been rained out, Huzoor, and it won't be possible to follow—but see this little edge of mud? That's made by a corner of a rubber shoe, and there's another just by it where a second man trod.'

'H'm, maybe so.' Bhimbahadur sounded doubtful, and Aitahang knew that the Corporal was not convinced.

'Well, just carry on.' Bhimbahadur motioned to Lalbir to continue. Aitahang was rather abashed, but cheerful; there were terrorists about somewhere—could they be from One-Eye's gang? For fifteen or twenty minutes the section moved on slowly and quietly then Aitahang suddenly felt danger. In front of him Lalbir stopped, and backed towards him, staring at something in front. Aitahang froze, heard nothing, then Lalbir waved him to get back, and at that moment the grey space beyond him moved.

'Elephant!' shouted Aitahang. 'Get aside!' He saw Lalbir turn, then saw the upswung white of a tusk, a curled trunk and pink throat and tiny furious eyes, then a huge head swung down and the tusk was plunged deep into Lalbir's body. With a jerk of his head the elephant shook off the body of the young Gurkha, and at that moment Aitahang heard from the distant deeps of memory a hoarse old voice saying in Limbu Kura, 'There's only one place to shoot an elephant . . .' He lifted his rifle and aimed at the central patch of forehead between and above the eyes. He shut out thoughts of everything but that saucer-shaped patch of grey hide, staring through the backsight, bringing up the tip of the foresight and gently squeezing his fist round the small of the butt and trigger, so smoothly that he did not realize the rifle had fired till the muzzle-blast stung his ears and he saw the elephant stagger. Its legs began to fold and slowly it crashed over sideways, in a tangle of snapped branches and flattened stems.

'Bren!' shouted Bhimbahadur, and cut his hand down in the order to fire.

'Hold it!' Aitahang waved them back. 'Don't shoot!'

'The scout—'

'Run through, but the elephant's dead!'

'Get Lalbir, drag him clear—come lad, easy now—' They kept glancing hurriedly at the twitching grey bulk beyond as they seized the body of the scout and half-stumbling, half-walking, carried him back a few yards.

'If that thing moves, give it a magazine!' gritted Bhimbahadur. Aitahang had never seen him enraged, but now the round placid face was red and furious. Kulbahadur stood between the carrying party and the elephant, bren gun at hip and finger on trigger. 'It's not moving,' he said hoarsely. 'It's dead.'

'Lalbir's badly hurt.' Carefully Bhimbahadur cut open the injured man's shirt and the soldiers fell silent as they saw blood welling from a deep puncture wound in his right-hand side. Bhimbahadur put a hand on his chest, then snapped out, 'He's still alive. Quick, shell dressing, vests—anything to pad this up and stop the bleeding.' Efficiently and without fuss the Gurkhas padded the great wound, tied the injured man's arms to his sides to prevent undue movement and began making a stretcher from cut poles and a poncho cape.

'We'll need help,' said Bhimbahadur. 'The others will be turning towards us, thinking we've surprised bandits, but they'll be moving quietly. We want 'em here quick. Thirteen,' he ordered, 'fire three rounds at five-second intervals—they'll realize we're in trouble.'

When the three rounds had been fired the section settled down to wait and, leaving the others to guard Lalbir, the Corporal took Aitahang to have a look at the elephant. They walked round the huge bulk of it, and Bhimbahadur said in puzzlement, 'Where did you hit it? I can't see any wound!'

'Middle of the forehead.' But kneeling in front of that massive head Aitahang himself had difficulty in locating the bullet-hole in the grey wrinkled hide, till an insignificant trickle of blood gave it away.

'I always thought these things had skulls thick enough to stop a bullet!' Bhimbahadur looked with doubt at the tiny bullet-hole. 'You must have got him right in the brain!'

Aitahang made no comment; he was himself intrigued by that flash of memory; there had been other things that had stirred in his memory once or twice recently, something to do with his home . . .

'*Manchhe aunchha!* Someone coming!' They crouched apart and lifted up their weapons. In a few minutes the slight rustle of leaves grew louder and they caught a glimpse of a canvas jungle hat with the battalion crossed-kukri sign stitched to it. Bhimbahadur whistled softly and the soldier approached, his rifle up, then stared in astonishment at the huge mass beyond, flies already buzzing about it. 'We met the bull elephant,' explained Bhimbahadur grimly, 'he got Lalbir.' The rest of the section came up silently, eyes questioning, looking in disbelief at the huge mound of grey hide.

As they moved back to see Lalbir, Aitahang heard a rapid, sonorous muttering in a tongue he did not understand. Several men stood gathered round the stretcher, with Bombahadur standing upright behind the injured man's head and praying in a low rapid voice. Occasionally Lalbir moved feebly but was held quiet by Kulbahadur and Kesersing. The low, incomprehensible prayer went on and on; no one stirred, but Aitahang felt the concentrated force of the half-dozen Gurkhas willing the injured man to cling to life. At length Bombahadur finished, moved away a few paces and sat down by himself. Lalbir lay quieter now, his eyes shut and breathing more steadily. Then the bushes rustled again and the platoon commander appeared among them, followed shortly afterwards by Three Section.

Quickly Lieutenant Narsing issued his orders. The three sections would take it in turns to carry the stretcher, make a track in front, and carry the packs of the stretcher party.

'The nearest place for vehicles is the tin mine,' he said. 'We'll report by wireless and by the time we're out there'll be an ambulance and escort there, and probably the battalion medical officer as well.'

For long hours they struggled through the forest, and by mid-afternoon emerged at the tin mine. Lalbir was still alive, but the long journey on the stretcher had set the blood flowing again, and he was very weak and white by the time the Medical Officer met them. At once he was given intravenous plasma, whisked into the ambulance and driven away.

The rest of the company had already come out at the tin mine and the Major was standing talking to the mine manager.

Aitahang looked about him. He had seen tin mines before, near the training depot, and this was very similar—great open expanses of gravelly tailings, a tall scaffolding for the water flow, half a dozen low mine buildings grouped inside a barbed-wire enclosure set with floodlights, and the tall forest all around. At one end, away from the mine buildings a little, were the village-like quarters of the Chinese mine-workers.

The mine manager, a middle-aged European with a sunburnt face and short moustache, turned to the Major and said, 'I've had some tea made for your lads—it's ready now at our cookhouse,' and nodded over to where the Malay guards were carrying out a large cauldron. Aitahang was weary, and drank the hot sweet brew gratefully, but was interrupted by a call from the platoon commander, who was talking to the Major: 'Thirteen! Over here!'

He put down the tea and hurried across, and the Major said quizzically, 'Killed many elephants before this?'

Aitahang smiled and shook his head.

'That was a brave action,' the Major said, seriously now. 'You saved the life of your leading scout, for the elephant would have trampled him.' He nodded dismissal, and Aitahang turned about and doubled back to his mug of tea.

'Was that the chap who killed the elephant?' asked the mine manager incredulously in a strong Dundee accent. 'What age is he, for goodness' sake? He looks to me as if he should still be at school!'

'No schools in the Gurkha hills, I'm afraid,' the Major replied. 'That young chap is down on our roll as eighteen—but that's only his official age, if you understand me.'

'I do, I certainly do!' the manager replied, shaking his head. 'He's tall enough—but I can tell, he's just a bairn!'

'Been wounded once already. He's not a child any longer.'

'Too young for this,' murmured the manager. 'Far too young—even for a Gurkha.'

The company set off along the track back to their base, passing one end of the mine-workers' village on the way. Aitahang glanced at the few Chinese who were visible, mainly women and children, but felt the pressure of eyes watching from the darkness of the huts, and wondered just how much these villagers knew about the terrorists in the forest behind and, if they knew, whether they dared speak.

'No use going back in there now,' commented the Major the next morning to the platoon commanders. 'That bit of elephant shooting has put every terrorist for miles on the alert. We'll let them settle down a bit, then try again. After Dasehra will do.'

'Any news of Lalbir?' asked Four Platoon commander.

'Wireless message this morning; he was operated on last night, and is still very weak, but he'll live. He owes his life to that youngster, Aitahang Limbu.'

'He does, Sahib.'

'I'll write Aitahang up, I think—the Commanding Sahib will want to know the details. Now, for the next few days till we have our Dasehra holiday we'll patrol to the west, just to see what exists in that stretch of mountain.'

While the officers were settling down over their maps Aitahang was reading two letters. The first contained good news, and was from Manbahadur, written in the rest camp at Penang. 'I will rejoin the battalion in two weeks,' he wrote, 'completely recovered. I hope to come back to B Company and will ask to come to your platoon.' He described how his chest wounds had healed up, and ended with wishes for Aitahang's safety. This was good news for Aitahang. Although he now felt that Four Platoon was his home and One Section his immediate family, yet it would be very good to have someone with whom he could talk of real home affairs. Many other men in the company had relatives serving with them, or the sons or brothers of neighbours; it seemed that only Aitahang had nobody. Manbahadur's forthcoming return was good news indeed.

The second letter, however, contained depressing news. It was from his father, who wrote, 'I have again seen the old Phedangba, and asked him to extend the time. But he has heard from the parents of Manbahadur how he was badly wounded, and that you too were wounded. The Phedangba says that he cannot wait any longer than a year. Another Limbu farmer is offering to buy the land. He says again that he is old—if it were anyone else he would not wait at all.'

The company spent that day preparing for further patrols to the western hills, and as he worked at his equipment Aitahang thought about his father's letter. It was only too clear that the old Phedangba thought he'd be killed before he could return with money for the land, and this news slipping out about his wound in the ambush only reinforced his opinion. He had less than a year now; it would be difficult to achieve, but—and he set his jaw—he would manage it somehow.

Thoughts of the encounter with the elephant kept returning, not only of the shooting, but of that strange trick of memory. It was funny how he had remembered that fragment of the old story-teller's tale after all these years; presumably the sight of those elephant tracks in the early morning had set his mind working. Aitahang felt not so much uneasy as unsettled; he kept feeling that there were other memories even further back which plucked at his mind, but when he searched for them they receded into the misty vagueness of childhood. It was curious, for they seemed to be mixed up with his thoughts whenever he made calculations about buying the land—and when he visualized the land again, picturing to himself that view across the Mewa, always somewhere in it was that cruel, one-eyed face, always just sliding out of the corner of the picture.

He didn't like it at all: distant stirrings from the past, the land, One-Eye, even the elephant! He sighed to himself; everything seemed mixed up—perhaps it would all resolve itself one day. All he could do now was get on with his patrolling, save money, and look out for One-Eye.

# 10 THE TIN-MINE GANG

'There we are, lads—that's where we're going this time,' said Bhimbahadur as Four and Six Platoons prepared themselves to set off. 'Gunong Besar Hantu. We haven't had a moment to patrol it till now.'

Through a gap in the ridge trees they saw to the west a strange high fluted cone of grey rock and green forest, a scarf of early morning mist still about its shoulders.

'It's high,' grunted Jagatman, 'and if you ask me it's too far for the bandits. They like their village comforts occasionally.'

'Not all of them, surely!' said Kesersing with his quiet smile.

'Not all of them,' agreed Jagatman. 'The really tough mobs stay deep. But these local scum here—' He spat carefully and relapsed into silence.

'You don't think this lot were the road ambush gang, then?' asked Aitahang as he charged his magazine.

Jagatman cocked an eye at him. 'You've a personal interest there!' He shook his head. 'I don't think so, different smell to 'em.'

'Fall in!' The platoons assembled were checked, and loaded their weapons.

'*Hin!*' They set off in single file out of the camp along the concealing ridge behind.

Later that day the Malay police officer in charge of the post at Manchis rang the company commander on the field telephone that connected them. 'I have some news,' he said carefully.

'I'll come and see you at once,' the Major replied, and called for the scout car. As soon as the driver had warmed up his engine the Major climbed in and they drove out on to the road and south the three miles past the tin-mine track entrance to the police post, and into the fortified enclosure.

'*Selamat pagi*, Tuan,' greeted the police officer. 'Come into my office, where we can talk undisturbed.'

Once they were comfortably settled, with cups of coffee in front of them the police officer said, 'I think we have an informer.'

'That's *very* good news! We haven't had a scrap of information about this area for a long time. Can you tell me about it?'

'It's a little difficult to be precise, Tuan, as the information reached us via one of the Malay guards at the tin mine. Anyway, this is what he told us. Yesterday night, while he was on guard at the perimeter fence not far from the mine office, a Chinese voice speaking in broken Malay called to him. It said that one night soon a ration party from the jungle would be coming into the edge of the mine tailings, to pick up sacks of rice made up by collections from each Chinese household.'

'Did he see the man?'

'No, it was too dark. These informers trust no one. He only said he would bring word of the time the same way, and that we were to wait in ambush at a place he would tell us.'

'What about the reward for him if this works?'

'As you know we pay only when the information brings results

—a thousand dollars for each dead terrorist, five thousand for known leaders, and as much as ten thousand dollars for badly wanted men. Then there are the payments for their weapons as well—a hundred for a rifle, and as much as five hundred for a bren.' The police officer smiled. 'It's a lot of money for a man earning fifty or sixty dollars a month. Anyway, you may be sure that he will hear exactly how successful any ambush is, and he will probably give us instructions about the money in the same way. We can hide it for him somewhere to pick up unobtrusively, or we can do it by numbered bank account—we must be very careful to keep his identity secret; dead informers discourage others!'

'Did he give any other information about the gang—how many there are in it, or who the leader is?'

'No, he said no more. He didn't want to risk staying too long near the perimeter fence, and in any case he will be able to sell us that information separately.' The officer smiled again. 'These Chinese workers have a keen money sense!'

'I have a platoon in base at the moment,' said the Major, 'and there will be one full section ready every night. Just telephone, and we can meet in darkness and make arrangements. In a few days' time we will be sending most of our men into Bentong to celebrate the Dasehra festival, but there will be a duty platoon and at least one officer left on call.' He drank up his coffee and rose to go.

'Thank you,' said the police officer, 'we may have some luck now. By the way, the guards at the tin mine say you had a man injured by an elephant.'

'Yes. He'll recover, though he was badly hurt. His life was saved when the man behind him killed the elephant.'

'An elephant was killed?'

'Yes. A pity, for the shot warned every Chinese bandit in the area that we were there.'

'Can you give me the map reference?'

'Certainly.' The Major looked at the map on the wall and wrote down the six-figure reference. 'Why do you need it? There was nothing there of interest.'

'I must tell the Game Warden at once. We have strict orders about this. If a rogue elephant has to be killed we must let him know, and usually he does it himself. That must have been the big bull that was destroying the fruit trees in Kampong Bahru.'

'I expect it was. Well, we've saved him a job.'

'Now *we* have a job. The Game Warden, as you know, is an

official of the Pahang State Government. What you may not know is that all game in the State is the property of the Sultan. The Game Warden will have to send in men to get the tusks and the feet, and I will have to provide them with an escort.'

'They'll have no difficulty finding the dead elephant—there's a big trail made by Four Platoon when they carried their injured man out. Your chaps'll be able to race along it. But you'd better get this done quickly, in case the bandits get the tusks first!'

Back at the company base the Major was given the wireless reports from the two platoons. They were approaching the slopes of Gunong Besar Hantu from different directions, and both reported absolutely no sign of enemy in the area. What seemed unusual, however, was the absence of any traces of enemy, old or new. Within a few days' march of inhabited areas there usually existed some sign of man's passing—a one-night bivouac, perhaps, where Chinese couriers had slept on their way to or from a forest base; a cut frond, or the old ashes of a cooking fire. But there was nothing, nothing human, that is, for the Gurkhas were coming upon many signs of wild animals.

'Pity we're not after *shikar*,' growled Jagatman at a break during the second day's march, 'there's everything here.'

'Curious,' commented Kesersing. 'Usually the game is in close.'

'Why curious?' asked Aitahang. 'Surely there's more in the deep forest?'

'Not in Malaya,' the other replied. 'It's because of the plantations. At home in the Gurkha hills we don't have forests growing right up close; as you know it's long ago been cut down for firewood or for house timber or by the charcoal burners, except up on the high ridges near the snow-line, so the game lives far away. But here the trees grow right in, up to the plantation edges. First of all the barking deer and the big red sambur come in to eat the bark of the rubber trees, and wild boar come in for the root crops, or for fallen coconuts. Many other animals do the same—porcupines, giant rats, squirrels, and—' he nodded at Aitahang—'elephants. Then you get the tigers living in close, too, to prey on the deer and the wild boar, so you don't have far to go to find game. But in the deep forest you seldom get much more than the tree-top animals—gibbons, and flying squirrels. Oh, yes, you get the seladang.'

'What on earth's a seladang?'

'It's a wild buffalo, six feet high at the withers and with short curved horns anything up to twenty inches round at the base, and tapering to points like needles. We sometimes see them, and we take care to keep well clear of them.'

'It *is* an unusual sort of area this,' agreed Bhimbahadur, 'not a sign of bandits—not a smell of 'em.'

'Reckon we're wasting our time here.' Jagatman sniffed and spat.

'*Kambar Kas!* Buckle your belts!'

That evening Four Platoon built its bivouac within the patrol area and well up the slopes of the mountain. When night fell the section observation posts were withdrawn and night sentries posted. From midnight Aitahang and Bombahadur sat together for their two-hour spell, occasionally passing whispered comments. 'Do bandits ever move in darkness?' asked Aitahang.

'Only in rubber plantations, where there are little paths between the lines of trees,' Bombahadur whispered back. 'It isn't really necessary to have sentries in the big forest at night—you wouldn't get five yards without getting tied up in thorns or falling into a nullah and breaking your leg, or tripping over a fallen branch and losing your weapon. But we all sleep easier with sentries on!'

For long minutes they sat on in silence, then Bombahadur spoke again in a soft whisper. 'We'll find no bandits here; you've probably guessed that.'

'Yes.'

'Do you know why?'

'No. But I don't like it.' Aitahang shivered briefly. He felt uncharacteristically depressed, almost guilty, as if he were engaged in something unlawful.

'Why do you think we see only the tracks of animals here, and not a single track made by men? This would be a good area for terrorists, but they have left it severely alone.' Bombahadur paused then went on, 'While you sit here do you sense anything?'

'No, Huzoor—at least, I'm not sure.'

'Wait then, and listen.'

The two Gurkhas sat motionless. A quarter of an hour passed, and still they neither spoke nor moved. In the complete blackness beneath the forest trees a leaf or two rustled in the night breeze, and here and there were small sounds—the tick of a beetle, from far away the metallic cry of a nightjar, an unidentified animal calling sharply, the rustle and whirr of tree rodents moving. It was as if the forest breathed quietly in its sleep. Long minutes passed and the two had sat immobile for nearly half an hour when Aitahang felt Bombahadur suddenly grow tense beside him, then his own muscles tightened and his breathing grew unsteady. Every sound in the forest stopped. Aitahang felt his heart thud loudly against his chest. Then a leaf or two rustled, the breeze sprang up again, a nightjar cried and the two Gurkhas let out their breath with deep sighs. Aitahang licked his dry lips. 'What was it?' he whispered, although he knew the answer.

'It was the Forest Man passing.'

'Here too? In Malaya?'

'Yes. He is here too.'

As the soldiers had predicted, not a trace of enemy was found on the mountain, and before the week was out they were marching back to base, all glad to be away. Puzzled by the complete lack of any sign of human activity whatsoever the Major mentioned this to the police officer a day or two later, when visiting the police post.

'I could have told you that your men wouldn't find anything there,' the Malay police officer replied.

'Why not?'

The police officer took down Wilkinson's *Malay-English Dictionary* and said, 'Look up "*Hantu*".'

The Major turned the pages: '"*Hajat*" . . . "*Hamis*" . . . "*Hampa*" . . . ah, here we are, "*Hantu*",' and read out, '"An evil spirit, a ghost or goblin; *Hantu Rimba*, the demon of the forest." So,' he said, handing the book back, 'Gunong Besar Hantu would be "Demon Mountain!"' He smiled wryly. 'That fits, all right; I know the men didn't like it there, and it usually takes something special to disturb Gurkhas. In fact it's about the only thing that *will* disturb them! By the way, anything from your informer?'

'Nothing yet.' The police officer frowned slightly. 'I had expected something from him earlier than this.'

'I'm taking most of the company into Bentong tomorrow for two days, for the Dasehra ceremony, but my second-in-command will be ready with an ambush party whenever you ring.'

'That's good, Tuan. Please say to your soldiers from us

"*Selamat Hari Dasehra*"!' The two officers laughed at the transposed Malay greeting.

'Thank you, I will.'

B Company's Dasehra party, which included Aitahang, reached Bentong by midday, and the men dispersed among the tents of H.Q. Company. Parties to celebrate the festival were coming in from all the rifle companies and space was short, but no one minded; a holiday atmosphere was in the air. Apart from standby platoons at the company bases everyone could forget about operations for forty-eight hours, and Gurkhas roamed the H.Q. area casually dressed and relaxed, looking for friends and neighbours and relatives. Rum supplies were plentiful and cheap, and gradually there rose the hum of hundreds of men chatting, with here and there groups singing to the high, ringing beat of a madal, the small hand-drum of the hills.

Rather aimlessly Aitahang wandered among the chatting, singing groups, not lonely, for there were sixty men of B Company scattered through them, yet feeling rather solitary, and this feeling was intensified when he heard a snatch of shrill, reedy notes. Someone was playing a shepherd's pipe and the sound stabbed at him. Should he not now be up on the high pasture with his flock? The first frosts would be coming, and the air so clear that he could see the snow-line on Topke a little farther down each day. In the farm-house below, his mother and father would be waiting for him, with Bhalu and Little Sister, and Balahang milking the cows, and above the byre his bear's fur would be ready in the hay. He had thrown it all away, and—he admitted to himself—he probably wouldn't be able to raise the money for the land in time to get it home before the Phedangba's deadline. He had left home for nothing.

Unusually despondent, but drawn by the shrill sound of the pipe Aitahang picked his way between the groups of men. The sound was coming from a quiet spot behind a tent, and when he looked he saw a soldier with his back to him, seated on the ground and playing to himself. Aitahang stood watching. He knew that figure, and when it paused for breath he leant over and said, 'Hullo, my friend.' It was Manbahadur.

After that the Dasehra holiday was transformed. They sat talking eagerly till the shout of '*Khana*!' and joined in the queue for a huge and very special meal of rice, curried vegetables and ducklings, paid for by the Battalion Fund; they watched the dancing which followed, themselves joined in the enormous Limbu harvest dance which started after ten and went on till just before midnight; and they went to the battalion temple, where exactly at midnight a black goat was decapitated with a kukri to prayers from the battalion priest. The two lads returned and joined in a fresh bout of dancing till nearly dawn, finally curling up to sleep exhausted till roused by shouts of 'Breakfast—nine o'clock!' when they had another fine meal. This Gurkha warrior-festival in honour of Durga, Goddess of War, was making a good start—but the tensest moment was to come, the sacrifice of the buffalo.

In the middle of the compound a stake had been sunk deep in the ground. As the soldiers massed around the stake the priest blessed a stand of weapons garlanded with flowers—half a dozen brens, dozens of rifles with bayonets fixed, kukris, swords, even a three-inch mortar mounted on its baseplate. At the same time goats were being led up and beheaded by several soldiers with razor-edged short kukris, and their carcasses dragged bleeding to a heap at one side.

Then the buffalo was led out. A rope round its horns was passed through a hole in the foot of the stake, and held by a line of men on the far side. The priest said prayers, signalled, and a powerful soldier emerged from the temple where he had spent the last days in prayer and meditation. He carried a great sacrificial kukri, its broad blade nearly three feet long, and as he reached the buffalo he put the kukri behind his back. The priest prayed again and sprinkled water on the buffalo. It shook its head as the water splashed on it, and the priest commanded, 'Cut!'

The line of men heaved on the rope, the buffalo's head was pulled down and the straining neck exposed, the man with the kukri swung it high over his head and, as the watching mass of Gurkhas fell silent, brought it down in a tremendous two-handed sweep. The horned head thudded to the ground and the headless carcass toppled over.

'A clean cut! A clean cut!' The watching men roared with relief: a botched blow would have brought twelve months of misfortune to the battalion—and many remembered one year this had happened, and the twelve months of toil and many casualties that had followed.

But this year it was indeed a clean cut, and as the Gurkhas

shouted the madals began their steady throbbing beat and a team of dancers leapt out and circled the stake and the bloody sacrifice.

'Here, lads—rum!' N.C.O.s with rum jars splashed big tots into the ready mugs, and the powerful spirit was downed like water. The soldiers, many still sleepy from the night of dancing, seemed to gain new life from this good omen, and among the tents and around the Headquarters building madals throbbed and groups sang their own songs of home. So went the day, with more feasting and rum in the evening, with Limbus, Rais and Tamangs dancing turn by turn. Night fell, lamps were lit and still the dancing continued; midnight passed and only when big drops of rain began to fall did they disperse to the crowded shelter of their tents.

Aitahang and Manbahadur had drunk no rum, but were very tired through excitement and lack of sleep.

'You're coming back to the company with us tomorrow? No, it's today!' asked Aitahang with a final tremendous yawn as he sleepily tried to pull his mosquito net away from a corner of the tent which was leaking rain in on him.

'M'm. Suppose so,' replied Manbahadur, 'but we'll hear in the morning—no one'll be doing much before we've eaten. It must be nearly two in the morning.' He yawned hugely and mumbled, 'Must sleep—sleep . . .'

Outside, the rain, which had started quietly enough, steadily grew heavier, and as they drowsed off the soldiers recognized it—a typical Malayan rainstorm, battering down with such force that spray rose from the ground. The night grew chill and a heavy mist formed and hung between the trees and clung in great beads of moisture to the tent ropes. The soaking canvas grew taut, and when an incautious hand or arm touched it, water dripped down. All sounds of revelry and rejoicing had ceased, and now all was still, with the stillness of exhaustion.

But in the wooden-floored section of the Headquarters building which served as the officers' mess a Gurkha signaller was going round with a torch, flashing it through mosquito nets to the sound of muffled and resentful comment from sleepy officers. 'B Company Sahib?' he asked, firmly ignoring all protests. 'B Company Major Sahib?' At last he found him, shoes off but otherwise fully dressed stretched out under a mosquito net and with a powerful aroma of rum about him. 'Major Sahib!' he whispered urgently. 'Signal *ayechha*.'

'G'way,' muttered the recumbent form under the tangled mosquito net. 'Tomorrow'll do—*bholi*, eh?'

'Police signal, Sahib,' said the signaller, and at that the Major sat up, rubbing his eyes.

'Let's see it.' He took the message form and the signaller held the torch so that he could read. With a muttered exclamation the Major sprang up and grabbed for his shoes. 'B Company duty N.C.O. *lai bolai deu!*' he ordered curtly.

Some twenty minutes later Aitahang opened his eyes reluctantly to a torch shining in his face. 'B Company man? Up you get!' The rain was drumming down on the straining canvas, outside vehicles were starting up and their headlights shone piercing beams among the tents. Aitahang peered up to see the duty N.C.O., cloaked in a dripping poncho cape, treading as best he could between the sleeping men, shining torches on their faces and asking, 'B Company? B Company?' Aitahang groped round for his boots in the dark till someone lit a hurricane lantern. 'All B Company men get ready. We go back at once!'

'What, now? In darkness?'

'Now. Come on, outside, quick as you can.'

Gradually, from odd corners throughout the H.Q. area, the B Company men assembled. Most were half-stupefied with rum and sleep but they stood in the rain and mechanically answered the roll-call. When they were ready with their bundles of bedding and their weapons the company commander addressed them, with the rain lancing down through the headlight beams.

'The tin-mine gang have struck while we've been away. They captured the mine, killed half the guards, got their weapons, murdered the manager and left the mine buildings on fire. That was about two hours ago. And,' he added to himself, 'they picked just the right time to do it.'

They reached the company base still in darkness but with the rain slackening, reorganized into their platoons and sections at once and prepared for operations. 'Four days' rations and straight off to the mine,' was the order. 'Five Platoon are there already.' There was no pause for food; as soon as their packs were filled they climbed back into the trucks and drove to the tin-mine track. 'They won't ambush us in the dark,' said the Major. 'Drive right on into the mine compound.'

The Chinese village was silent. Not a light showed, and even though the sky was paling in the east not a soul stirred. Five hundred yards away it was a different story. The wreck of the mine buildings smouldered, the fires extinguished by the rain. The air was bitter with the smell of half-burnt wood, and Malay police from the Manchis post and the surviving guards were hunting through the wreckage in the growing light, searching for missing weapons and equipment. The smoke-stained Malay police officer greeted the Major morosely, and gestured without a word to a line of blanket-covered bodies. 'The Tuan manager and four of the guards,' he said bitterly, 'and I know where those bandits came in—they got up close through the Chinese village.'

'Likely enough. Can you prove it?'

'What's the use? The Chinese workers would only say they heard nothing till the shooting started. In any case, they couldn't have done much.'

'We'll set off after this gang as soon as we can. Five Platoon are out looking for tracks now, and as soon as they find something we'll go. Nothing from your informer?'

'Nothing. Perhaps he was deceiving us.'

'Perhaps. Curious way to go about it, though.'

The two waited as the grey sky paled into a clean, washed blue. The soldiers sat quietly against their packs just outside the cut gaps in the barbed wire and the Major, yawning, saw that a number had dozed off. His own eyes felt weighted with lead and his mouth was dry and sticky. He pulled out his waterbottle and drank deeply. That was better! He wiped his mouth and rubbed his eyes. The police officer, looking at him sideways, said, 'You seem a little tired, Major.'

'Dasehra is a busy time, too busy for sleep. But the omens are good this year, the omens are very good.'

The police officer looked at him in surprise. 'Good, you say? I hope our luck will be better than this!'

'Major Sahib!' There was a call from beyond the wire. A soldier was walking quickly from the forest edge a hundred yards away.

'They've found something.' He swung on his pack.

The soldier approached and spoke in Gurkhali, and the Major turned back to the police officer and said, 'I think you ought to come and see what they've found.'

They crossed the gravelly tailings and followed the soldier into the trees. Five Platoon commander stood there impassively. He saluted. 'We've found tracks, Sahib, about twenty men. But they left something else for us to find,' and he pointed.

Beside the fresh trampled trail left in the soft earth by the terrorists was a man tied to a tree. He was wearing fragments of the blue clothing of a Chinese workman. He was dreadfully mutilated, and dead. The Major looked away, and caught an expression of horror and disgust on the face of the police officer. 'You know who that must be,' he said.

'Yes. The informer.'

'Someone must have seen him coming away from the perimeter fence by the guard post that night.' The Major shook his head. 'Pity—we'll have to start again just tracking. If only he'd told us all he knew—however, we'll be off. I'll have our base send you any news we have.'

'Get them!' said the Malay officer vindictively. 'Murdering swine!'

With Five Platoon sent back to base to wait in reserve, the company commander and Four and Six Platoons set off hot-foot along the trail. One of Six Platoon sections led, so Aitahang had no chance to study the enemy footprints before they were trampled into oblivion by the feet of the Gurkhas ahead. He was not concerned, however; many men of B Company were experienced trackers, even though he knew in himself that they could not approach his skill; and the trail left by the enemy seemed quite clear and fresh.

His main worry was lack of sleep; at every brief halt he felt his eyelids droop, and at midday, when the Major ordered a half-hour halt for a hasty brew of tea and a mouthful of biscuit and tinned fish, Aitahang and several others not on sentry found themselves dozing off.

'They seem to be heading south-east,' said the Major as he plotted their progress on his map with the two platoon commanders. 'We've crossed this ridge east of the mine, turned south a little here, then down along this long spur and along the side of this valley.'

'They'll be going pretty near the end of that Malay kampong if they keep this up,' said Lieutenant Narsing. 'It's a big area, though.'

'Surprised they didn't split up after the raid,' said Five Platoon commander thoughtfully.

'Perhaps they're over-confident, this lot.' The Major sat poring over his map, trying to suppress his yawns. He had slept little over Dasehra, and felt as he were struggling through cotton-wool. 'All we can do is follow as fast as we can.'

Next to lead off was Four Platoon, with Two Section in front. They had travelled less than three hundred yards farther along the trail when, as the leading scout was crossing a small stream between two low ridges, a rifle banged out at him. He ducked down and opened rapid fire back and the men behind threw off their packs and charged, fatigue forgotten. '*Ayo!*' they shouted. '*Ayo! Ayo!*' and with a rush they burst into a camouflaged sentry post.

'Straight on!' A beaten path wound back from the sentry post and they raced along it. 'Here's the camp!' They charged into a group of tall huts in a circle round a beaten-earth parade-ground. It was quite empty.

'Spread out! Four Platoon right—Six Platoon left! After 'em!'

The running men spread outwards and began hunting through the trees, eyes looking everywhere for signs of the escaping men. 'Keep looking!' urged Bhimbahadur to his section. 'They'll be off like bloody jackals!' He mopped his face angrily as he and his section ranged about. They were now well out from the camp, and where a few moments ago the forest had seemed full of charging Gurkhas, now it seemed to have swallowed them up. A little way off on the right flank Aitahang felt as if he were quite alone, with no one for a hundred miles, although he knew that others of the section were no more than thirty yards away. All about were interposing tree-trunks, with curving, head-high thorn fronds in between. It was just then that he found the footprint.

He examined it carefully, for it could have been one made a day or two earlier, but it was fresh; he saw from the delicate, uncrumbled edges of the shoe-mark, and the clean indentation where the toe of the shoe had pressed in deeply—the sign of a man running for his life—that it was newly made. He followed the line of it, found another print a good yard farther on, spotted where the running man had torn his way past a thorn frond, then saw an exposed root roughly scraped. There was no doubt: one man at least had run this way from the camp in the last minute or two.

He called quickly, 'Got one's tracks, over here.' Corporal Bhimbahadur hurried over to him, and Aitahang knelt and showed him the successive prints.

'H'm,' nodded the section commander, 'they're new all right.'

'And look,' said Aitahang in excitement, 'here—a second man!' A little farther over to the right was the sharp imprint of a different shoe.

Bhimbahadur glanced at his compass. 'They're going back north-west. I'll tell the Lieutenant Sahib and we'll get off after 'em.' He was replacing his compass in his pouch when they heard the whistle of recall from the direction of the camp. 'They've found something,' he said. 'Come on—leave this lot.' The section followed him back to the camp at a run, to find the others gathering in the open space in the centre of the group of huts. There were quick orders: a big, fresh trail had been found leading south-east on the far side of the camp.

The section commander then reported: 'Two men, Huzoor, running north-west,' but the platoon commander explained, 'There are tracks of a dozen or more going the other way—both platoons are to follow them. It's probably the main party. Forget the two.'

While the remainder of the sections gathered Aitahang snatched a moment to examine the Chinese camp. He looked hurriedly, with certain suspicions in his mind. He started going from hut to hut, but was interrupted. 'Come on, One Section, let's go!'

Five Platoon led off again and followed the trail at a great pace, and again Aitahang had no opportunity to study the tracks before they were obliterated. He thought with regret back to the fresh tracks of those two men: hunting those would have been more in his line; this rush down a well-trampled trail seemed too easy. More than once, however, the company commander stopped to check their direction with map and compass, and the last time he summoned the platoon commanders. 'The trail's swinging more and more south,' he said, frowning. 'If we continue along this line we'll come out into the rubber estates below Manchis, and you know what that means.'

The two Gurkha officers nodded. They knew, all right: once in the rubber plantations the terrorists' tracks would mingle with those of the rubber tappers. They would get clean away.

'We haven't got too far to go,' said the company commander, 'but I'm afraid they'll be there before us.'

Events proved him right; the Gurkhas still had not caught up with the terrorists when they emerged into the rubber trees late in the afternoon.

'That's it, then,' said the Major with a sigh. 'They've got away.'

He blinked wearily. 'God knows where they are now. We'll get back to base and get some sleep. Signaller,' he called, 'open your set. I'll have the trucks meet us at the nearest bit of track. In the meantime, platoon commanders, put out sentries and rest.'

Aitahang lay back against his pack in the warm shade of the rows of rubber trees, trying to stay awake. Not far away Manbahadur, now the platoon commander's runner and escort, made no pretence—he was sound asleep. Aitahang felt his eyelids drooping, but something held him awake. There was something that nagged at him, and at last he got up and walked back to where the tracks they had been following met the rubber plantation. He saw with disappointment that only the diamond-soled markings of Gurkha jungle boots remained, but he walked back a little way, eyes on the ground, and was eventually rewarded by finding a portion of print left by a rubber shoe. He knelt and examined it very carefully, exclaimed to himself and hurried back to his section commander.

Corporal Bhimbahadur listened, at first sleepily, then with growing attention. 'Come on,' he said, 'we'll tell all this to the platoon commander.'

'Well, what is it?' Lieutenant Narsing asked.

'It's that camp, Huzoor, and the tracks,' said Aitahang a trifle awkwardly, hoping he wasn't about to make a fool of himself.

'Go on,' said the officer encouragingly, 'tell me what you think.'

'Well, Huzoor, as you know we found very fresh tracks of two men running fast round to the north-west, but the main trail led south to here.'

'Yes?'

'I've just looked at a print on this big trail, and it is at least a day old.' Aitahang saw doubt in the officer's eyes and added, 'I am quite certain of that.'

'So,' said the officer, 'that means that the main party of enemy were not in the camp when we found it—only a couple of men! The others had set off and made this trail down here a day earlier!' He spoke in a puzzled voice.

'And, Huzoor,' Aitahang continued, 'there had been men enough in that camp yesterday—but it had not been slept in for months.'

'I must tell the Major Sahib at once.' Lieutenant Narsing scrambled to his feet. 'If what you say is correct, then something peculiar is going on.'

'Well, now—let's think,' said the company commander when he

had heard Aitahang's report. 'There are a number of peculiar things about this. First of all, as we know very well, bandits *always* split up after an ambush or some attack or other. They never leave a trail to follow if they can help it. Yet this time they not only left a trail but obligingly left it leading right up to their sentry post. Then, when the sentry fired, instead of scattering as they always do, they again obligingly all seemed to run off in single file, till they came out into the rubber and vanished.'

'It's certainly odd, Sahib,' said Lieutenant Narsing.

'It is indeed—but one thing now explains it all. Your lad says that the trail we've been following is a good twenty-four hours old, maybe a trifle more. If he is right—and I have no reason to see why he should be wrong—we now know exactly what the enemy did. They made this trail *before they attacked the mine*! This is to keep us busy looking in the wrong direction! If it hadn't been for young Aitahang Limbu we'd be spending the next fortnight combing every bush and tree from here south to the Negri border.'

'Maybe, Sahib,' said Five Platoon commander cautiously. 'Maybe.'

'Maybe nothing, Sahib—I tell you, it all fits now. Ten minutes ago nothing fitted.'

'But what about the sentry who fired? And he wasn't alone!' The platoon commanders were a trifle sceptical; this sounded just a little too clever.

'Don't you see, Sahib, there *had* to be a sentry to fire a shot—otherwise how could we be bluffed into thinking that the others had just run out the far side?'

'And the second man?'

'Oh,' and the Major laughed, 'he was to see that the first man didn't run off a bit too soon! You know these Chinese—they never trust each other, especially the Communist ones!' He grew serious again. 'And that camp would have been one of their old ones. You know how they up sticks and move every so often, usually to puzzle their own supply people as much as anything just in case of treachery!'

'Well, Sahib, it sounds possible,' said Lieutenant Narsing cautiously. 'In that case, where is their *real* camp?'

'Ah—that's going to be the difficulty, Sahib! Now, the footprints of those two men, where did that lad's section commander say they led—north-west?'

'North-west, Sahib.'

'Well, that's back towards the tin mine again, but I expect they were just running in a half circle to get right round behind us, as we charged off in the wrong direction. That sort of thing would appeal to them, and would suit them very well—ourselves and them going fast in opposite directions. No, it won't be north-west because of the mine, but it could easily be north-east!'

'That sounds like it, Sahib.'

'Now, let's just look at the map for a minute.' The Major pondered over the map, then said, 'I've got a hunch. Do you see this low spur here? It's about five map-squares north-east of the mine—that's three hours' travel if you know exactly where you're going, and double that if you don't. It has a small stream running by it, quite enough water for any number of bandits, but—and here's why I'm looking at it—there's a belt of swamp behind it a thousand yards wide. Once into that and they'd be safe. In that watery mess tracking is impossible. I'll bet the camp is on that spur!'

'Yes, Sahib, it could be there,' said Five Platoon commander, 'but if it *is* there it will be a difficult place to attack. They'll have the forward width of the spur covered, and will break back into the swamp and get away.'

'Not if we attack them from the swamp!' Fatigue forgotten, the company commander was busy poring over the map, and then he looked up, eyes narrowing. 'We'll give them tricks! Now, this is what we'll do . . .'

# 11 SWAMP ATTACK

When the company trucks arrived Four and Six Platoons drove back to the company base, passing through the village of Manchis on the way. 'The Min Yuen here will send a runner into the jungle camp to say we've packed up and gone home,' said the Major quietly to the men in his vehicle, 'and the uniformed gang will reckon we've been very thoroughly fooled.'

The Gurkhas with him hid their smiles, and one, a suspicion of a twinkle in his eye, said, 'They'll just get an even bigger surprise in a day or two!'

'Well . . . maybe,' said the Major. 'We've been hopeful before, and often enough it's come to nothing. We must just keep trying.'

That night all but the sentries were asleep early, many too tired to do more than snatch a mouthful of food before their eyes closed. The company was shaken awake again at four o'clock in the morning, but with eight hours' sleep they were men refreshed —and vengeful men too, vengeful with terrorists who had taken advantage of the Gurkhas' main festival to commit dreadful atrocities, and to try to make fools of them into the bargain.

Once again shouldering their heavy packs the two platoons slipped into the forest in darkness, not far from the track leading to the mine. 'No one can have spotted us,' said the Major as they sat inside the first trees waiting for daylight. 'We'll separate at first light and march round. You, Sahib—' he nodded towards Lieutenant Narsing Limbu—'and your platoon will come with me on the approach through the swamp, and Six Platoon will spread out in front of the spur, in two-man cut-off groups. We'll get into position today and close in tomorrow. Usual wireless drill.'

After a long march the two platoons slept that night in the forest not far from their approach lines to the spur—Six Platoon well to the west of it, in case they were heard, or their footprints found by terrorist patrols, and Four Platoon and the company commander east behind the swamp. At first light they spoke by wireless. 'Take up ambush positions,' the company commander ordered Six Platoon. 'Listen for Four Platoon's attack.'

For Four Platoon the march through the thousand yards of swamp was no march at all, but a slow, dragging struggle through a wilderness of mud, water, tall swamp trees and especially vicious thorn bushes, the pale, inch-thick stems studded with thin, sharp spikes. Each step had to be felt for in the knee-deep liquid, in case a root tripped the unwary into those waiting thorns, and sometimes deeper patches were found, usually by the leading scout disappearing up to his chest, when he had to be hauled out by the men behind. Normal marches in forest were bad enough, with the burden of heavy pack, weapons and ammunition; in this swamp it was a nightmare.

Progress was so slow and difficult that by midday the company commander was beginning to wonder if they would be out of it by dark. Map-reading was impossible in this featureless stretch, and he fixed their position by dead reckoning. From the first everyone was soaked through and plastered from head to foot with swamp mud, and many had acquired painful thorn gashes, but they struggled on without complaint. They all knew from bitter experience that only those who took enormous care and trouble could hope to surprise terrorists in forest.

At last, at three o'clock in the afternoon, a whisper came back to the company commander, 'Dry ground.'

He halted the platoon and went forward. The scouts pointed. A little way ahead was the welcome sight of trees growing in solid earth, the hated pale thorn bushes replaced by the dark green fronds of the ordinary forest. 'Go very slowly forward,' he whispered to the scouts. 'See if there's anything immediately in front.'

In a few minutes the two scouts returned, and crouched by him, their faces tense. 'Smoke,' they whispered. 'Just a faint smell of it, a little way ahead.'

The Major's heart leapt—his hunch had been right! He beckoned forward the others and whispered, 'Packs off, spread out, very slow now.'

For some minutes they lay flat against the gently rising slope, both resting after their exhausting swamp journey—during which they had been unable to take off their packs and rest—and also listening for sounds of men. They heard nothing and the Major signalled for a cautious advance. Moving very carefully and stopping every few yards to listen they went forward through the trees in a line, and at last they were rewarded; a human voice came to them, from no more than forty yards ahead, and there, suddenly, was a narrow beaten path. The Major signalled: 'One Section—move left of the path; Two and Three this side!'

Would there be a sentry on this path? More cautiously than ever they moved forward, drifting through the trees like mud-stained ghosts, till the forest gloom lightened fractionally in front of them where smaller trees had been thinned out. Again they heard voices, very close this time, the incomprehensible sing-song of a Chinese dialect, and at last saw the outlines of steep, atap-roofed huts.

'One Section—extend to the left!' signalled the Major again, and Bhimbahadur and his men were just beginning delicately to move sideways when there was the bang of a rifle-shot, a moment of shocked silence, high yells of dismay, a burst of carbine fire, the boom of a shot-gun and the heavy rattle of a bren.

'*Ayo!*' roared the Gurkhas and charged straight in. A shot-gun boomed again, and rifles opened up at them, but were silenced by Two Section's bren.

'They're off!' On the left Aitahang had a quick impression of numbers of men in khaki, scattering away through the trees at great speed, some hatless, others clutching weapons, and all running as hard as they could.

'After them!' One Section began to run in pursuit when short rapid bursts from a light automatic began spraying amongst them.

'Where's that coming from!'

'Can't see!'

The terrorist was firing from behind one of the big trees at the edge of the enemy camp, sheltered by its enormous buttresses, and he was only given away by the faint haze of smoke that stood out above him when he fired.

'There he is! Get round behind him!'

The men of One Section continued their dash to the left to out-flank him, but Aitahang, noting the exact spot from which the Chinese was firing, thrust forward his safety catch and fired one round. Splinters of wood and bark flew up, and as the Chinese ducked back Aitahang ran towards him. Round the tree again came the fat slotted muzzle of the tommy-gun, a head in a red-starred cap squinting behind it. Aitahang fired once more from the hip, then as the terrorist wavered he raised his rifle to his shoulder, and took deliberate aim through the ring sight, ignoring the yellow flashes which began to sparkle out at him from the tommy-gun. He ignored them, and the jerk and clatter at his hip, where his water-bottle was shot through, and squeezed his trigger.

There was a violent clang of metal as his bullet struck the metal breech of the tommy-gun, shattered the steel cocking handle and spun into the terrorist's forehead. His head snapped back, the tommy-gun tumbled forward and he vanished behind the tree. Aitahang rushed forward again, but one glance at the sprawled body was enough.

There were one or two more scattered bangs, then shouts of 'Hold on—steady on there, Six Platoon's not far ahead!' In and around the camp the shooting stopped, and for a moment there was an uneasy silence.

'All right, Thirteen?' called the section commander. 'He nearly got you, that one!' His round face was set in a fierce grin and he looked more ferocious than Aitahang had ever seen him.

'I'm all right,' he called back, rather shakily, 'I need a new water-bottle!' His chest was going up and down in great uneven breaths now that the immediate danger was past and he fingered the jagged metal and torn webbing on his hip where the terrorist's bullets had smashed their way through, trying to shut out from his mind the thought of what they would have done to him had the Chinese had another moment to aim. He glanced back to his right, into the circle of huts. One dead terrorist with a shot-gun across him lay stretched out near one of the huts, and in the middle of the huts a soldier of Two Section stood with his shirt ripped off and another man binding up his shoulder, bleeding from half a dozen buckshot wounds.

'Spread out again! Advance!' The company commander waved and the sections began moving forward along the spur beyond the camp. Almost at that moment they paused to listen. Some three hundred yards farther on a roar of firing suddenly erupted all across their front.

'They've bumped Six Platoon—come on!'

The men of Four Platoon plunged through the trees and in a few minutes were waved down by the two-man ambushes of Six Platoon. 'Some got through!' shouted Six Platoon commander.

'Right! Get your sections after them—Six Platoon forward and left, Four Platoon forward and right. Come on!'

But it was obvious that the terrorists, running for their lives, had scattered all through the forest. Only an organized search would achieve anything, and the Major returned to the spur and whistled the recall. 'We'll start a proper search in a minute,' he said to the two platoon commanders. He stood for a moment wiping sweat and mud from his face. He was gasping for breath after running through the trees, but filled with the peculiar elation that comes to those who are still on their feet after a fight. 'How many d'ye get, Sahib?' he asked Six Platoon commander.

'Don't know yet; here, runner, pass a message, get those bodies brought in here quick!'

'We got two in the camp and had one man wounded,' said the Major. 'That was the tin-mine gang all right.' He was getting his breath back, and holstered his pistol. 'It worked. We were lucky.'

'Well . . .' replied Six Platoon commander, 'it wasn't *all* luck!'

The company commander nodded. It had indeed been very

much more than luck—but that could all be thought about later. As soon as the bodies were counted and the weapons collected organized pursuit must be mounted.

The bodies of the men killed by the Six Platoon ambush parties were being dragged in—two, three and then a fourth, and Aitahang looked at them intently—but One-Eye was not among them. He leant on his rifle, head bowed; if One-Eye had been there he had escaped. He was beginning to feel a wave of reaction.

'Aitey—are you all right?' It was Manbahadur, hurrying over to him, looking worried. 'You're not hit?'

'No, I'm quite all right.' He straightened up and looked at his friend. This would never do, this surrender to fatigue and despair. 'But how about *you*? How are those wounds of yours?'

Manbahadur looked tired, and rather ill. 'That swamp was bad.'

'Over here—give us a hand!' There was a call from a short distance away. 'One still alive!' Half a dozen men ran off and returned in a few minutes carrying on a groundsheet a badly wounded terrorist. He had been struck in the thigh by a bren-gun burst, and was bleeding heavily. 'Get a tourniquet on him, that's it; put a fist on the pressure-point in his groin, that'll stop the blood.' The platoon medical orderlies quickly checked the bleeding, injected a syrette of morphia into his arm and gave him a drink of water.

'Too late,' said the company commander, 'pity—he'd tell us a lot if he lived.'

The dying man was ghastly pale, and looked in apprehension at the hard Gurkha faces above him. Aitahang saw that he was a terrorist of no particular rank, for slung about him was an old-fashioned leather bandoleer of rifle ammunition in clips of five. It certainly was *not* One-Eye—and then he had an idea. 'Major Sahib,' he said, 'can you ask him something for me?'

The company commander looked up to see Aitahang. 'Oh, hullo there, Thirteen. You got one today, I saw! But what do you want from him? Anyway, I can't speak Chinese.'

'The Major Sahib speaks Bazaar Malay.'

'A little.'

'Most of the Chinese speak Bazaar Malay. Ask him, Huzoor, how many eyes the gang leader has.'

'What! How many eyes—!' The company commander stared.

'Yes, Huzoor, how many eyes.'

'Very well!' Puzzled, but beginning to grasp the significance of the young soldier's question, the Major said: '*Orang jahat kepala berapa mata?*' and indicated his eyes. The dying man gazed back at him blankly.

'He doesn't understand, Huzoor,' said Lieutenant Narsing. 'Some of these terrorists only speak Chinese.'

'I'll try again.' The Major repeated his question, this time seeing an answering flicker. The dying terrorist whispered something and a Gurkha put his ear down close to him. 'What does he say?'

'Huzoor, he says "Two eyes".'

Aitahang was both disappointed and relieved—disappointed that One-Eye was elsewhere, and relieved that at least he had not been in the camp and escaped. That would have been almost too much to bear.

It was late afternoon, and the company commander decided to bivouac on the spur and begin organized patrols on the morrow. He saw that Four Platoon in particular were weary—a good night's rest in a properly-made and comfortable bivouac would get them back to their fighting fitness once again, so he gave the welcome order, 'Make camp!'

While the groundsheet shelters were being put up Aitahang noticed that the company commander was taking photographs of the dead terrorists, having them dragged to where the forest shade was lightest and the dead heads carefully pillowed on logs—taking as much care with his camera and exposure meter as a society portrait photographer. The Gurkhas saw this activity with relief, for it would save an exhausting struggle back with the dead men on poles. The bag had been a big one—of the twenty or so terrorists in the tin-mine gang six were dead and one wounded and captured. The rest would spend the next few nights in the open forest, hungry and frightened, not knowing when a Gurkha would rush at them through the trees, until at last they contacted the Manchis Min Yuen for food and shelter. That night the total of dead rose to seven when the wounded man died.

'Seven out of twenty, Sahib—that'll stop their nonsense for a while,' commented the company commander to Four Platoon commander that evening.

'They really will clear out now, Sahib,' said Lieutenant Narsing with a smile. 'No tricks this time!'

'That young lad Aitahang Limbu's the one we mainly have to thank, Lieutenant Sahib.' The company commander thought for a moment. 'First the elephant, then this bit of first-class observation—as well as killing a bandit and nearly getting killed himself in the process—I've a good mind to put him in for a decoration!'

'He deserves it, Sahib.'

'I'll write him up when we return. Now, there are a good dozen of these swine left, but they'll be well scattered by this time. Let's have a look at the map . . .'

For two more days the platoons searched through the forest, but the survivors made good their escape. Aitahang was able to follow one set of footprints for several hundred yards, but they then vanished in another heavy downpour of rain. At last, out of rations, they returned to base, where an escort party had already taken the wounded Gurkha and the terrorists' weapons and documents, and the Major's spool of film. The soldiers arrived to a double issue of rum, a huge meal of hot rice and meat, and the announcement of three whole days of rest while Five Platoon took over the search, extending the patrols far to the south.

'Clean up, lads—make and mend, that's the order!' Bhimbahadur led his section down the hill the next morning with their filthy clothes and mud-engrained webbing to the sunshine of the open paddy field by the cookhouse and the stream. There they revelled in unlimited flowing water, scrubbing their uniforms and webbing and spreading them out to dry on the short bushes by the forest edge, then returning to the hill-top to sit cleaning and oiling their weapons, checking ammunition, inspecting grenade primers, refilling their containers of leech-repellant—a host of small, necessary tasks.

At length they were finished and Aitahang found himself in the unusual position of having nothing to do, for the first time in many days. He did not relish this, for his mind kept returning to the problem of the money and the land, and the more he thought about it the more he began to understand that time would run out before he got the money home. He stretched out on his blankets in the section hut, gazing up at the thatched roof and endlessly turning the same facts over and over in his mind. If only he had more pay—if only he had more time—if only . . .

'Hullo—is Sixty-Six Thirteen in there, Huzoor?' called a familiar voice. It was Manbahadur. 'Ah, there you are, Aitey—doing anything?'

'Nothing at all!' called back Aitahang, jumping up in relief at his friend's appearance. 'Let's walk down the hill. Got your rifle?'

The two friends wandered down through the clumps of bamboo and came out to where the washing was drying behind the cookhouse. This gave the camp a homely look, heightened by the faint drift of blue smoke from Harkadhan's cookhouse. The sun felt warm on their skins, very welcome after the shady gloom of the forest, and the peace of the morning was only heightened by the sound of bird calls and the musical quavering of gibbons from the wooded ridge above.

'Not a bad place, Malaya,' commented Manbahadur looking about him, 'when we get a chance to see it!'

Aitahang did not answer and eventually Manbahadur said, 'You're very quiet. What's up?'

'Oh, I don't know. Can't seem to settle, somehow.'

'Perhaps it was that killing the other day.'

'No, it isn't that.'

'Sorry you joined up?'

For a moment or two Aitahang made no reply, then said rather sadly, 'I won't manage the land money. Looks as if I needn't have joined up at all.'

'Listen,' said Manbahadur forcefully, stopping and gripping his friend's arm, 'this is the only way you or I will ever get land of our own before we're middle-aged men. Whether it's one piece of land or another doesn't really matter in the end. If we hadn't joined up we'd be landless shepherd-boys still.'

Aitahang sighed, but nodded. 'I expect you're right.' In his heart, however, he still longed for that land across the Mewa—it seemed to haunt his thoughts, as if it were already part of him.

'But there are other things than land,' Manbahadur went on. 'Don't you remember how restless we both were, how we talked continually of adventures in foreign lands? Isn't that part of the reason for joining? And,' he said shrewdly, 'haven't we both learnt a lot?'

Manbahadur was right, of course, Aitahang admitted. There *were* other things than the land, many other things—the adventures, hard and dangerous though they were; the broadening of his outlook; the increased knowledge of his own countrymen and the wonderful spirit of comradeship with everyone in the whole battalion, from the Colonel downwards. He smiled. 'Come on,' he said briskly, 'we'll go for a quick walk, then back up to our huts and write home again. It's a month or two since we've sent off a letter, and there will still be leave parties going from Jalapahar!'

While the two friends were talking the Major was receiving an old friend, a very pleased Malay police officer. 'I didn't think that even the Gurkhas would find this gang!' he admitted with a smile as they shook hands.

'Please come in and sit down, Enche,' said the Major. 'We've no coffee, but I'll send for an orange for you from the company canteen. I'll stick to beer!' He gave a shove with his foot and the police officer looked under the G.S. table to see half a dozen bottles of beer cooling in a bucket of water, and laughed, 'You've worked for it!'

For some little time they spoke of operations, discussing possible regrouping areas for the escaped terrorists and the chances of getting another informer to give them some news. 'Not very likely now that the locals heard what happened to the last one,' said the police officer with a grimace. 'I'll try publicizing these rewards a bit more.' Eventually he rose to go, then exclaimed, 'I nearly forgot—I have something for you.'

'Yes, what is it, Enche?'

'It is not for you, actually, but for two of your soldiers. Do you remember the elephant your soldier shot?'

'Yes, of course.'

'We took in the Game Warden and one of his men, following the trail your men had left. It was too late to get the feet in proper condition, but of course the tusks were all right—and they were beauties. The Game Warden's man cut them out and took them back to the Sultan, down in Pekan at the mouth of the Pahang River. He was very pleased with them, and was most interested in the story. He has sent rewards for your men. Here they are,' and the police officer took a folded wad of red ten-dollar notes from a waterproof folder. 'He asks that the wounded man and the man who shot the elephant each receive a hundred dollars.'

'He is very generous!'

'Ah, he is fond of Gurkhas—all we Malays are! Will you see that the men get it?'

'I'll have this paid into the injured man's credits in the Battalion Fund, but the other man is here, I'll give it to him now. No—*you* give it to him, say it's from the Sultan. He's a good lad, and he got one of the tin-mine gang himself, the chap with the tommy-gun.' The Major stuck his head out of his hut. 'Line orderly! Give a shout for Sixty-Six Thirteen.'

Manbahadur and Aitahang were climbing the long zig-zag of steps up to the huts when they heard a cry of 'Thirteen! Sixty-Six Thirteen—Koi! Where are you?' They set off running uphill as fast as they could. 'Quick,' ordered the Line Orderly, 'the gaffer's calling.' Aitahang hesitated. He was in trousers, vest and gym shoes and was bare-headed. He felt that he should go and dress properly. 'Never mind that,' said the N.C.O. impatiently, 'go as you are; don't keep him waiting.'

The police officer stared as a young lad ran up and stood to attention in front of the company commander. 'An elephant, and then a terrorist with a T.S.M.G.!' he murmured to himself, really surprised, but said aloud in Malay, 'From the Sultan,' and handed Aitahang a wad of the ten-dollar notes.

Aitahang stood looking from the notes to the police officer to the company commander, who hurriedly explained: 'That elephant you shot; the Sultan has the tusks now, and he has sent you a hundred dollars as a reward.'

Aitahang stood looking down at the money, quite stunned with surprise. He had never held so much money in his hand in all his life; it seemed like a gift from heaven. Then realization began to flood in on him. A hundred dollars—that was well over a hundred and fifty rupees! He could send it home at once by a leave party; it meant that by the monsoon he would have enough money after all! He stood thinking back to the elephant—and then of Lalbir, impaled on a tusk for which he was now being paid. He stood wordless.

'That's all, Thirteen,' said the Major. 'If you want to put that in the Battalion Fund or send it home, see that the Captain Sahib gets it straight away; he'll see to it for you.'

Still Aitahang did not move and, rather surprised, the Major said, 'Is anything the matter?'

'Huzoor,' Aitahang looked up at him and held out the wad of notes, 'you must send this to Lalbir Tamang. He was badly hurt.'

For a long moment the Major looked at the young lad with the big rifle, giving away more money than he had ever had in his life, then he said gently, 'It's all right, lad,' picked up his haversack and took from it the other red packet. 'Lalbir was not forgotten. This is his. That money,' he nodded at the bundle in Aitahang's hand, 'is all for you.'

'*Hunchha*, Huzoor!' acknowledged Aitahang curtly. He turned about smartly, paused and strode away, his face a disciplined, expressionless mask, but inside him his spirit was soaring higher than the white peak of Topke, as high almost as that great dark peak with the snow plume, in the country where no birds fly.

After the rout of the tin-mine gang patrolling remained an uneventful affair for B Company for many weeks. November slipped into December, when the Malay rainfall took its yearly upsurge. 'Not as bad as the monsoon in our Gurkha hills,' grunted Aitahang to Manbahadur after a particularly wet spell of patrolling, 'but enough to get on with,' and gradually they dried out in January. With no terrorists to engage their weapons the company commander ordered that more hunting parties go out, and every day pairs of men with rifles stalked among the abandoned paddy fields and overgrown belukar jungle around the company base, and there was much fresh meat with their meals of rice—usually the lean meat of a wild boar, but occasionally venison from a barking deer. Once Aitahang tracked and shot a sambur, the big red deer of Malaya, and the Major had the horns sawn from the skull and nailed above the small company office hut 'for good luck'.

During this period Aitahang saw his first Malayan aborigines, the Sakai.

On their way back to base after a day patrol One Section came upon a group of little reddish-brown people, nearly naked, walking solemnly in single file beside the road. Aitahang had heard of Sakai from others in the section, but had never actually encountered them, and he was fascinated at their diminutive stature, which gave them a deceptively childlike appearance, and their seven-foot-long blowpipes, the six-inch long darts carried in a delicately woven quiver of cane.

They stopped as Bhimbahadur waved to them, but did not smile or show any change in their expressions. Aitahang felt that they were not unfriendly, just not concerned with these heavily-armed, broadly-built Gurkhas in their faded green uniforms. One thing they asked for by signs was cigarettes, and the two smokers in the section, Bombahadur and Jagatman, offered them cigarettes from the round tins of fifty they carried in their pouches. Aitahang could not help smiling at Bombahadur's disconcerted face when the leading Sakai, instead of taking one cigarette, calmly took the whole tin and stowed it away in his basket—but Jagatman kept a firm grip on his and allowed the Sakai only one cigarette each. 'They're not as stupid as they look,' he observed caustically, 'and I'd like to know just when they last saw Chinese bandits in that forest of theirs!'

In the other company areas, though, sporadic patrol fighting took place—but the terrorists' main activity seemed to be directed at establishing a rule of terror over the civilian population. Hardly a week went by without the murder or disappearance of someone suspected by the terrorists of not being wholeheartedly on their side—or who had refused to pay them subscriptions or to give them food. The Gurkhas were intrigued to learn that these victims were all Chinese, and gradually came to understand that not all Chinese supported the terrorists. In fact, they discovered, most Chinese were heartily sick of them—but the secret rule of terror was stronger than the distant influence of the Government. The only way to relieve this situation was through the death of terrorists—but over the B Company area hung an uneasy peace, and the soldiers began to feel a strange, guilty boredom. 'I never thought that we'd be sorry to have peace and quiet, Sahib,' grumbled the Major to his Gurkha Captain, 'but what we need is some action.'

'Don't ask, Sahib,' said the Gurkha officer cautiously, 'we may get rather more than we want!'

Then at last came news of terrorists, though not in B Company's area.

Farther north local Malays reported the appearance of armed and uniformed men among the rubber estates half-way from Karak to Temerloh, and the Gurkha company based near Karak set off hot-foot the dozen or so miles north-east to see if they could hunt them down. This news arrived with the routine situation reports at B Company base on a morning in mid-March, and the company commander read it with some irritation. 'These D Company fellows are getting all the luck,' he grunted.

'That's what they were saying about us, not so long ago,' the Gurkha Captain said with a smile.

'Too long, I'm afraid, Sahib,' the Major rejoined. ''Fraid we just won't get anything more down here.'

That day the returning B Company patrols only confirmed his opinion: a series of sweeps through the forest on both sides of the main road, and a long sortie into the hills east of the mine—for the dozenth time since the action—brought the same news: no tracks, not a sign of fresh movement. 'I'll go and have another word with that police chap tomorrow,' the company commander told his officers. 'He may be able to suggest something.'

But that visit was never made. A signal was brought to the Major the next morning early as he was shaving in front of a steel mirror hanging from a nail outside his hut. 'Hang on a minute,' he mumbled through the soap on his face, 'I'll look when I've finished.'

'It's important, Sahib,' said the signaller dryly.

'Whatever it is I'm going to finish shaving.' He brought the razor carefully round his cheek and jaw, under the chin and back again. 'There,' he said, rinsing his face and rubbing himself dry with a towel, 'now I can deal with anything.' He opened the sheet of message pad, read the brief contents once and then again and nodded to the signaller: 'Send an Ack.' He dried his razor, folded his towel and packed up his shaving kit in a worn sponge-bag and walked without haste to the company office. 'Duty N.C.O.,' he called. 'Pass a message to all Platoon commanders: 'Stand by to move; four days' rations.'

He took the signal from his pocket and read it again. It said: 'Karak police post over-run first light this morning stop all defenders killed stop enemy escaping south-east stop Baker Company will pursue acknowledge.'

It looked as if he need complain of inaction no longer.

# 12 ON THE TRAIL

The company commander set off for Karak at once in his scout car, leaving the company to follow as soon as they were ready. More details of the action came in by wireless, and as the men filled their packs and checked weapons and ammunition the platoon commanders passed on the news as they worked. 'Must have been quite a large gang,' said Lieutenant Narsing. 'That Karak post was well defended.'

'Anyone know how many?' asked one of the men.

'No, we don't know a thing about them,' the officer replied, 'they seem to have appeared from nowhere.'

Busy ramming square 24-hour ration tins into his big pack Aitahang pricked up his ears. Where had he heard that phrase before?

'Any terrorists killed, Huzoor?' asked Bhimbahadur.

'No bodies found, though that doesn't mean much; they'd soon hide their dead, and they'd leave any wounded near by for the Karak Min Yuen to see to. But they must have been efficient, and pretty ruthless too, for they killed every policeman in the post, all fourteen of them.'

'But what about the police wounded?'

'There were no wounded.'

'There must have been wounded, Huzoor,' protested Bhimbahadur, 'especially as the police were fighting a defensive action!'

Aitahang knelt motionless by his half-filled pack, waiting for the answer he knew was coming.

'The wounded had all been finished off,' said the platoon commander. 'A single pistol shot each.'

Aitahang completed filling his pack, then he spread out his webbing equipment and removed the issue kukri from its leather frog. He untied his kitbag, delved deep into it and pulled out his long Limbu kukri. He bound the soft leather of the scabbard with a broad strip of olive-green drill cloth, and pushed it carefully into the frog. He then drew the blade and tested the edge, nodded to himself and replaced it in the scabbard. Something made him turn his head. Bombahadur Sunwar was watching him. Their eyes met, but neither spoke.

They caught up with the company commander at the police post just beyond Karak, and the Gurkhas stared round at this latest piece of terrorist activity. The dead police lay in a row covered with groundsheets, with beside them Malay women from the police married quarters, wailing for their dead husbands. Inside and outside the police post lay evidence of a severe action—trampled cartridge cases, bloodstained field dressings, a long smoke stain up one wall. The place was swarming with police reinforcements, home guards with shot-guns, the manager of the rubber estate and his guards.

'This time they came up through that lallang grass over beyond the rubber smallholdings,' the Major explained to the three platoon commanders, 'and it looks as if they went back that way, crossing the road south-east through Bukit Dinding rubber estate.'

'If that's the line they took they'll be into the Kemasul forest by this time,' said one of the platoon commanders, gloomily, 'then we'll have a chase!'

'I don't know,' said the company commander slowly. 'That

may be the line they started on—but is it the way they're really going?'

They looked at the map he spread out. 'The trouble is,' he went on, 'they could travel in any one of three directions from Karak, either south-east into the Kemasul Forest, south-west into the hills round Bukit Pabunga—and remember that our ration convoy was ambushed going past that stretch—or, a bit more difficult for them, they could strike north and cross the Sungei Bentong and the Sungei Klau into the Lakum Forest, even carrying on up to Gunong Benom.'

'It's a far cry to Benom,' grunted Five Platoon commander. 'My bet's the Kemasul Forest.'

'Too obvious,' commented Six Platoon commander. 'There's too much flat jungle there. They'll make for the hills, this lot, the steep hills beyond Pabunga.'

'What do you think, Lieutenant Sahib?' the Major asked Four Platoon commander.

'Well, Sahib,' he replied after a short pause, 'which is the direction that is going to be most difficult for us?' He looked round challengingly. 'You tell me that—and I'll tell you which way they went.'

'There isn't much doubt about that, I'm afraid,' the Major answered. 'Once they're into that Benom massif they're safe. It'd take twenty battalions to hunt them down. Look at it! Nothing but huge peaks—Pallas over 5,000 feet, Lebah nearly as high, and Benom itself only a few feet short of 7,000! And they're steep, too—full of rock faces and waterfalls. So you think Benom, Sahib?'

'Well, towards Benom, anyway,' Four Platoon commander answered cautiously. The other two Gurkha officers shook their heads, unconvinced. 'Too far for their food supplies,' growled Five Platoon commander.

'I agree,' added the other officer. 'They'd go for the hills, all right, but south-east—Benom's too distant.'

While the officers pondered, Aitahang sat with the rest of the company in the shade of the near-by rubber trees. He now knew for sure that this was the work of One-Eye's gang; it had the same complete, murderous efficiency about it as the ambush—and the way they had decoyed away the Karak company showed thoroughness and planning. It was One-Eye all right. Aitahang heard the N.C.O.s mention the trampled lallang grass with the trail leading south-east into a rubber estate across the road from the Chinese village, but this did not unduly concern him. He knew instinctively where they had gone—north towards the blue mountains of the Benom range. For One-Eye, nowhere else seemed appropriate.

'Section commanders!' The platoon runners signalled for the N.C.O.s, and the platoon commanders separated and gave out their orders. The section commanders then returned to their sections and gave out their own brief orders. 'The company's to split up and search for tracks by platoons,' said Bhimbahadur. 'Five Platoon's going across through Bukit Dinding to look along the forest edge there, Six is going south and then west of the road, and we're crossing the river and going north. The first platoon to find the real tracks will call up the others. Till then Company H.Q. will be at Karak.'

Four Platoon were ferried across the Bentong River in shallow dug-out canoes supplied by Malay fishermen. Once out of sight of the river the platoon commander called up his section commanders. 'The enemy went south-east into Bukit Dinding,' he said, 'but if they've come north they must have swung round to cross this same river farther east from here. Now, let's work out times.' They squatted round his map as he pointed out routes with the pointed tip of a palm frond. 'They attacked the police post at first light—that's just about six-thirty. They didn't take long; covering fire from three or four brens and tommy-guns, rush in, shoot the survivors, collect the rifles and ammunition and clear off again, attempting to set fire to it as they left. That would take about twelve or fifteen minutes, no more. Then they set off as fast as possible, laying the false trail. By heading south-east before turning north they had much longer to go to reach the river, say an hour and a half. That brings us to eight-thirty. What time is it now?'

'Just after ten, Huzoor.'

'We must reckon they're across the river, by now, and are an hour and a half on their way, going fast. If we march east parallel to the river and two or three hundred yards in from it, we will cut across their tracks.' He stood up and buttoned his map-case cover. 'They probably crossed no more than two thousand yards east from here.' He looked about him and up towards the ceiling of tree-tops. 'Getting darker; we'll have another of these damned thunderstorms later on. Let's go.'

A low ridge running east and west between the two rivers gave them an unexpected opportunity to make good progress, for a faint game trail ran along the crest of it, and Aitahang found himself forgetting One-Eye briefly as he spotted the tracks of sambur, barking deer, tiny mouse deer, pig and once the familiar pug marks of tiger. But they reached the end of the ridge where it dipped down towards the junction of the two rivers without finding any tracks of men, and the platoon commander halted in puzzlement. 'I could have sworn they'd cross the ridge,' he said. 'They *must* have come this way to get to the Lakum Forest today! If they had carried on farther east they'd reach the Malay kampongs round about Jambu Rias, and they wouldn't risk that—not having just slaughtered a dozen or so Malay policemen!'

'Perhaps,' said Two Section commander, 'they haven't come this way at all.'

'Maybe,' agreed the platoon commander. He muttered, half to himself, 'I could have sworn they'd head north.'

Then Corporal Bhimbahadur suggested, 'They'd have been wary of that game trail. Suppose they guessed we'd search along it?'

The platoon commander nodded. 'They'd take precautions. They would split up and cross it singly, to leave no traces on it.' He thought for a minute, then said, 'It's worth a try.'

While the rest of the platoon rested, two men without their heavy packs were sent back to search along the hill flank north of the ridge. They had been gone no more than five minutes when there came a long whistle.

'They've got it!' The platoon commander was jubilant. 'Here they come now.' The two Gurkhas came trotting back through the trees.

'They met up a hundred yards down the slope, Huzoor, there's a big trail.'

'How many are there, d'you think?'

'Huzoor, there are many—there must be forty of 'em.'

'That's all right, there are twenty of us.' He turned, 'Signaller, open your set, get me Company H.Q. in Karak.' In a few minutes he was speaking to the company commander, giving him the map reference of the tracks, the estimated number of the enemy and their direction.

'Good for you!' The company commander's voice came clearly through the headphones. 'Follow as fast as you can. I will call in the other two platoons. Press on!'

'*Hunchha!*' While the signaller untied his aerial and closed up his set the platoon commander called the section commanders. 'Once they're into the Lakum Forest plain they can scatter and meet up again in the Benom area, and we'll never find them. About half a day's march due north is a big patch of swamp, the headwaters of two big streams. They won't go in there, it would slow them down. They'll keep to the dry ground, for speed.' The three N.C.O.s sat studying their maps and listening. 'There's high ground on either side of the swamp, and it's my bet that they will make for the western ridge. It's very high and steep, going two thousand feet nearly straight up, but it's closer, and the Lakum Forest plain begins on the far side of it. Once they cross that ridge they're safe.'

'So we're to catch them up before they cross the ridge?'

'If we can. Tell your sections, then we'll go, Three Section leading.'

In a few minutes they were off, and five minutes later had reached the trampled line of footprints left by the gang. 'As fast as you can go,' ordered the platoon commander, 'and if we bump 'em—straight in!'

The trail led due north, and in twenty minutes of fast walking the leading section halted and sent back a message, 'River.'

'That'll be the Sungei Klau. Send two men over, and cover them across.'

The river was fast, waist-deep and muddy, but no more than fifteen yards wide, with the branches of the giant trees on either side meeting overhead. While the two scouts were slipping down into the water the rest of Three Section moved forward to the bank and propped themselves against trees, to watch the far bank. Holding their rifles above their heads, straining against the current with the water tugging at their packs, the two soldiers slowly waded across. The leading man had reached the far bank and was reaching for a handhold to heave himself up when a sharp burst of automatic fire broke out from a few yards beyond the bank. He fell back into the water, turned over once or twice in the current and drifted downstream, a reddish stain spreading out around him. The second man, caught waist-deep in the stream, fired one shot with his rifle, then he too was hit and collapsed.

'Fire!' The covering section opened rapid fire with bren and rifle but a hail of bullets crackled back at them from the invisible enemy and two more Gurkhas fell. The bren-gunner sprayed a full magazine across the river, and while he was firing a soldier jumped down into the water, struggled through the current, seized the nearer of the two scouts by his webbing, and dragged him back to the bank. He was still breathing, but bleeding hard from a big shoulder wound. Of the first man there was no sign.

'Get across there!' roared the platoon commander, and under cover of the bren firing rapid bursts over their heads Gurkhas jumped into the water and began wading across. The enemy fire ceased abruptly, and by the time the soldiers had reached the far bank and scrambled up the enemy rearguard had gone.

'One's been hit!' called out a man from Two Section. 'Bloodstains here, by these cartridge cases!'

'Follow on, but watch out!'

Tense, with safety catches pushed forward, three men hurried along the trail. 'Here he is!' They spread out. A khaki-uniformed figure lay across the track. 'He's still alive! Watch out—he may have a grenade!' Their warnings were unnecessary; the Chinese was very badly wounded, and lay gazing at them stonily as they approached. 'He's a bad one! Look at his face!' One of the Gurkhas quietly drew his kukri. 'I'll cure him of that.'

'No—he won't last long.' As they watched him he shuddered, choked and died. 'Looks as if the bren got him.'

'Where's his weapon?'

'Gone. The others'll have taken it.'

The platoon was reforming, and two men were sent downstream to look for the body of the first soldier. They found him caught against a tangle of driftwood in an eddy of the river, and pulled him back through the water. 'He's dead, Sahib,' they reported.

'See to the wounded, section commanders. Signaller, open the set. They'll have heard the shooting, and will be calling us.'

Sure enough, as soon as the set was switched on to the company frequency they heard the Company H.Q. signaller calling them: 'Hullo One, report my signals, over.'

Rapidly the platoon commander reported, ending: 'We'll be off after 'em straight away. I'll leave the wounded here for you to evacuate.'

'The other two platoons have just arrived here,' answered the company commander, 'we'll be up to the river in an hour and I'll bring police to evacuate the wounded. You crack on and we'll race after you, over.'

'Roger, Wilco, over.'

'Good luck. Over and out.'

While a police party was hurriedly being organized to go with the two Gurkha platoons, the Major telephoned the latest news through to the Battalion Intelligence Officer at Bentong. When they had finished the Intelligence Officer said, 'We have a message for B Company, just come in.'

'What is it?'

'Gurkha Brigade H.Q. at Seremban have just signalled us the latest list of awards. One of them is a Military Medal for a chap of yours, number Sixty-Six Thirteen.'

'Oh, I'm glad that's come through. That lad's off with Four Platoon, I'll pass a message when things quieten down a bit. It'll have to wait till then, he's probably pretty busy just at this moment!'

Aitahang was indeed busy. Four Platoon were hurrying along the trail as fast as their muscular legs would carry them. They well realized that they were up against the most determined terrorist gang they had yet faced, with all the advantages of initiative and opportunity, yet it only spurred them on. The platoon commander glanced at his watch. It was eleven thirty. That short action with the enemy rearguard had not only caused the loss of valuable men, but had wasted time. 'Step out, lads,' he called. 'Keep walking.'

Still easily following the big trail they began to find themselves on steadily rising ground. In spite of the steepening hills they only paused to change the leading section at intervals, then pressed on again. They wasted no time, for in this hilly country Gurkhas could outpace Chinese. It was shortly after one o'clock when One Section again took over the lead, with Jagatman as leading scout. Rifle tucked under his arm and jungle hat pulled down over one eye, he set a storming pace along the trampled line of footprints, and the platoon commander began to hope that they might even catch up with the enemy by nightfall—when once again the tearing rattle of a tommy-gun broke out ahead. A splatter of bullets cut through the leaves and Lieutenant Narsing dashed forward to see Bhimbahadur and Aitahang rushing forward over the body of Jagatman. There was a final tremendous burst, then three khaki figures broke away from behind a great fallen tree and ran in different directions. Bhimbahadur's Owen gun chattered out at them and one fell—but the other two dodged and ducked and twisted away, vanishing into the thickets of thorn fronds.

'After them!' The leading section threw off their packs and raced forward, while above them the darkening sky opened and heavy drops of rain began to fall.

The platoon commander knelt by Jagatman and turned him over. He was stone dead, shot through the heart. The rain pattered down on to his dead face, and the platoon commander picked up the fallen jungle hat and put it under Jagatman's head, so that it looked as if he were sleeping. One by one the soldiers returned, chests heaving, panting and enraged. 'They got away.'

Worse was to follow. 'Those two ran in different directions,' Bhimbahadur reported, 'away from the line we've been following.'

'We'll just have to forget them, and carry on after the main body.'

'That's the trouble, Huzoor—the trail's vanished.'

'What!' Lieutenant Narsing hurried forward with the N.C.O.

'See, Lieutenant Sahib? This is where they waited. There's no trail beyond it at all, only one or two footprints of the ambush party. Looks as if they've lost us.' As they stood staring at each other in the deepening gloom there was a flash of lightning, a pause, and with a rumble of thunder the rain poured down.

As he stood with water streaming from the brim of his jungle hat the platoon commander's thoughts were sombre. Of his strength that morning of twenty, two were dead and three lay wounded back at the river, with a soldier left to guard them. Including himself there were fourteen men on their feet, one of them a signaller burdened with a wireless and armed only with a revolver. Ahead were nearly three times his number of terrorists, heavily armed, on familiar ground and fresh from a successful battle with the police. In addition they had twice shown a murderous sting in their tail.

Yet the thought of waiting for the rest of the company to catch up never entered his head. He was worried for one reason only, the delay in finding the tracks. The drenching rain would soon wipe out what traces there were, and the Chinese would once again vanish in the forested slopes of Benom. 'Section commanders!' he ordered curtly. 'We will search again.' He turned to Bhimbahadur. 'Send two men beyond that fallen tree. That may be our best chance.'

Corporal Bhimbahadur nodded, mentioning briefly that in Jagatman they had lost their most experienced tracker.

'Don't forget that youngster of yours,' reminded the platoon commander shrewdly. 'Remember that he spotted that business with the tin-mine gang's tracks.'

'Of course, Huzoor. I'll take him myself.'

Behind the fallen tree there was a confusion of footprints, but Aitahang quickly saw that they were no more than the prints where the three terrorists had moved about when choosing their positions. Superimposed on them were the diamond-pattern prints of the Gurkha jungle boots. As he examined the Chinese footprints Aitahang described the men to Bhimbahadur, who listened in astonishment. 'There was one smallish man, very light on his feet, armed with a carbine.' He bent and picked up a short .300 cartridge case. 'See this? From an M1 carbine, I should say, and here is one of his prints, small foot in a gym shoe, a clear but shallow impression.' He stooped again. 'Now this was a larger man, he was firing a rifle, for here are two .303 cases, absolutely brand new.'

'He's the one I knocked over, then,' said Bhimbahadur, indicating the sprawled body with the Number 5 Lee-Enfield jungle rifle lying beside him. 'That's a new police rifle.'

'Now this third man who was here, he was the one who did the damage. Here's where he rested his tommy-gun on the tree-trunk; you can just see the tiny dents made by the barrel cooling rings on the soft bark, and over there, eight to ten feet back and slightly to the right, are the ejected cartridge cases. We must look out for him!' He spoke with a cold rage. This man, who had killed Jagatman and probably Two Section's leading scout at the river, was now marked down along with One-Eye for revenge.

'What's he like?'

Aitahang narrowed his eyes, moving his head from side to side to let the weak light show up the shape of the prints left by the man's feet, the impressions of his knees on the ground and the faint marks on the bark where he had rested his weapon. He wanted to get a mental picture of him, and as he studied the ground he spoke slowly to Bhimbahadur: 'He was of medium height for a Chinese, but heavy and thick-set—you see the very broad outline of this rather short shoe? His feet have actually bulged out the canvas uppers wider than the rubber sole. He should be easy enough to recognize.'

The N.C.O. looked at Aitahang curiously, noting the implacable tone of voice and the hard, determined expression. At first he had been rather doubtful about this lad's tracking ability—thinking that perhaps the tin-mine gang affair had been luck combined with a bit of intelligent observation. But this careful, reasoned explanation from the faintest of insignificant traces was convincing enough. 'Any sign of the others?' he asked.

'Not a sign.'

'But if the main body of the terrorists didn't come on here, how the devil did we lose them?'

'I think I know, Huzoor.'

'Well?'

'For the last two or three hundred yards before the ambush they would have stepped aside, one by one, leaving the ambush party to continue the final set of footprints up to the fallen tree.'

'But Jagatman would have spotted that the trail was diminishing!'

'Yes, he would—but not at once. Remember we were going fast, only studying the trail occasionally. He was shot before he had time to notice.'

'Come on, we'll tell the Lieutenant Sahib.'

The platoon commander listened in fury and frustration. 'We'll have to search outwards to find their rendezvous—it'll take hours!'

'Huzoor,' said Aitahang diffidently, 'there's one set of prints beyond the fallen tree of a heavy man—I think I can follow him.'

'Can you, by Shiva!' The platoon commander jumped up. 'We'll try it!'

'It'll be slow, Huzoor.'

'Never mind, you lead on. And Corporal!'

'Huzoor?'

'Keep Thirteen well covered. Have the bren ready not too far back, and a rifleman watching. He'll be too busy tracking to look out for himself.'

Beyond the fallen tree Aitahang cast round to find the heavy man's prints, and for a moment or two was unsuccessful, while the rest of the section and the platoon commander watched rather doubtfully. Then he straightened up with a grunt of satisfaction. 'Got him.'

The platoon commander came forward. 'Where? I can't see anything.'

Aitahang showed him a fragment of bark on the ground.

'That's from that fallen tree,' he explained. 'It caught on something like a magazine pouch, and then dropped off here as he was running off. This must be the line the man took. If we go along it we'll find more. Yes,' and he stooped again, 'this is the same line and here's something else, just a little scrape, but it could have been made by a shoe.' With the platoon commander following and watching, Aitahang went on, murmuring to himself, '. . . scrape on that rock . . . some bruised moss . . . a leaf squashed—aha!' At his exclamation the officer stopped short. 'What is it?'

'Footprint. The heavy man. See?'

The terrorist had momentarily been careless in his flight and had trodden hard on a patch of softer earth. The short, broad print was quite clear. 'It's deep,' commented Aitahang. 'He was running hard. He'll have left more farther on.' He straightened up. 'It should be quicker now, Huzoor.'

'Good for you, lad. This man will lead us to the rendezvous.'

'Maybe,' said Aitahang cautiously.

'He will,' said the officer confidently, 'and there's another thing in our favour; when the terrorists split up and scatter to hide their tracks they lose time as well. Now, Thirteen, lead on!'

The tracks led uphill, for now they were well into hilly country. Ahead, although they could not see it for the trees about them, rose the great ridge between them and the Lakum Forest, the ridge of Kaling. They began toiling up the approach spurs to the ridge, Aitahang ahead with his eyes on the ground, most of his attention on the job of tracking, but realizing full well what had already happened to two leading scouts that same day.

Higher and higher they climbed, leaving the warm air of the plains behind them, with all the time the hill spurs getting steeper, the trees slightly farther apart, the earth thinner and the rocks mossier. The single tracks of the terrorist turned, twisted, briefly followed animal trails and then stepped aside from them, and once ended at a narrow rushing stream so that Aitahang had to hunt along the banks for some minutes before finding his trail again, doubling back on the same side. Like a hunted animal this terrorist seemed to sense from well ahead that he was being followed. But in spite of all his efforts and cunning Aitahang followed every twist and turn like a bloodhound, and at one point he stopped and observed to the platoon commander, 'We're gaining a little on him.'

'How do you know?'

'We were held up nearly twenty minutes by that last ambush.' He held out a tiny piece of broken twig. 'This caught on his tommy-gun sling swivel or some such projection. See where the bark has been torn? Normally this type of twig discolours visibly inside half an hour. There is no sign of that, it is still quite white.' He tossed it aside. 'I'd say he's no more than fifteen minutes ahead.'

'You still all right to lead?'

'I'm all right.' Aitahang's only thought was for the killer of Jagatman, probably only a few hundred yards in front. Without another word he set off again, climbing steadily, but had hardly gone eighty yards when he stopped short and ducked behind a tree. From behind, Bhimbahadur crouched forward to him and Aitahang whispered without turning his head, 'The rendezvous.'

The Corporal put his hand behind him and beckoned, and Narsing came up silently and stared past them. In front was a small natural clearing among the enormous trees, a clearing made by a great tree toppling over and dragging smaller ones with it in a huge tangle of grey-white trunks, with above them a hole to the sky through which shone the cloudy light of late afternoon. To one side of the tangle the soft mossy earth had been much trampled, and the footprints were sharp-edged, new and fresh.

Without a word the officer gestured left and right, and from behind him the sections slipped round on either side of the clearing. A silent minute passed then the section commanders appeared at the clearing edges and signalled all clear. Quickly sentries were put out on three sides to listen, while others inspected the tracks, trying to count the number of terrorists. 'What do you make of them?' the platoon commander asked Aitahang.

'We're close; I'd say they moved out of here as soon as that tommy-gun bandit turned up—and that's now about twenty minutes ago.'

'Twenty minutes!' muttered the listening men. 'They're less than half a mile ahead!'

Lieutenant Narsing glanced at his watch. It was nearly five o'clock in the evening, and the light was beginning to fade under the trees. He thought for a moment. He could camp here and spend a comfortable night under shelter, and be ready for any further exertion in the morning—or he could press on until dark. That would mean a miserable night huddled in groundsheets on the soaking earth, and the hill air was already turning bleak and chill. The Chinese would also have to stop and camp by dark, and if the Gurkhas went on too far they might blunder into the enemy sentries and spoil everything.

But he paused only a moment before ordering, 'Carry on till it's too dark to move or see!'

Quickly his intention was passed by wireless and an encouraging reply was received. The rest of the company with the company commander, who opened his set for a minute or two every hour on the hour, were not too far behind, and following their tracks easily.

'Are you still going to be all right to lead?' asked the platoon commander in some concern, and Aitahang replied with quiet assurance, 'Quite all right, Huzoor.'

'Stay alert,' warned the officer, and Aitahang nodded briefly as he led off.

Although the light was fading steadily Aitahang kept up a rapid pace. Individual footprints were no longer distinguishable, but the enemy trail showed up as a darker line in the gloom, and he kept on until at last the line and the forest floor merged into shadow. He stopped. 'It's too dark to see, Huzoor,' he whispered. 'And I can hear water ahead.' The line of men stood listening, and faintly through the dark trees heard the steady boom of falling water. They knew the import of that water; somewhere along it the enemy were probably even now making their camp, and a sentry would be sent well back along this same trail, to listen for following troops.

'We've come quite far enough,' Lieutenant Narsing told the section commanders in a low voice. 'Put out one sentry per section, we'll sleep where we are. Last sentries to shake us up at five-thirty, an hour before first light. We'll try and catch them before they leave their night camp. No cooking, and remember—keep absolute silence, speak only in whispers.'

The Gurkhas pulled on their woollen jerseys over their wet shirts, for as soon as they stopped moving the chill struck into them, but soon their teeth were chattering. 'There's going to be a mist up here tonight,' said Kulbahadur, 'I can feel it in my bones.'

Sprawled beside him Aitahang did not answer. He was exhausted. Much of the day he had been tracking, straining his eyes for the slightest sign on the ground and never relaxing—and all the time he knew that if he caught up with his quarry his first warning would be a burst of bullets from the same tommy-gun that had killed Jagatman. The strain had been wearying, and hunger was like a dull pain inside him. He thought sombrely of the certain battle in the morning, and in spite of himself his mind turned towards the homely farm-house above the Mewa Khola, a hot supper cooked by his mother, Bhalu the dog beside him and the bearskin rug waiting in the snug hayloft. Icy drops splattered down on to his groundsheet as the evening breeze rose briefly, shaking the tree-tops, and he shivered. He felt cold and lonely, and a little afraid.

'Tsss!' He looked up at a whisper. 'Tsss—Aitey, are you there?' It was Manbahadur. He hissed back softly and his friend groped through the dark and sat beside him, huddling his groundsheet round himself.

'*Chiso*,' muttered Manbahadur, 'it's freezing!'

For a while the two boys sat in silence as the darkness closed in and the evening beetles sank into silence. 'When's your sentry-go, Aitey?' asked Manbahadur.

'Ten till midnight. When's yours?'

'Last; four till five-thirty.' He sighed. 'We'll catch up with them in the morning,' he murmured, half to himself. 'That'll be due to you.'

Aitahang did not reply. He felt light-headed with hunger and weariness.

'D'you know,' Manbahadur went on, 'this last bit of mountain-side reminds me of that stretch across the Mewa from your place—big trees, good water . . .'

He only received a sleepy mumble in reply and whispered contritely, 'I'm sorry, you must be all in. But here, this is what I really came for,' and in the darkness he pressed something into Aitahang's limp hand, something smelling of onions and chillies. 'I had this in my mess-tin, I always carry a little spare ready to eat. Take it, you'll feel better.'

Aitahang began to murmur in protest, but Manbahadur silenced him, whispering, 'You may have to do some more tracking tomorrow.'

Aitahang obediently stuffed the compacted handful of cold rice and vegetables into his mouth and gulped it down. He blinked with heavy eyes and licked the last of the rice from his fingers. By Shiva he was hungry! But that mouthful made him feel a little better and, somehow, less gloomy. He blinked again and leant his head back.

Manbahadur whispered, 'Feeling better?' but there was no answer. Aitahang was fast asleep.

## 13 BATTLE BY THE FALLS

'Up, lads, and quiet—not a sound!' It was still dark as the last night sentries shook their comrades awake, but gradually the outlines of gigantic tree-trunks began to take shape, looming up through the mist like pillars in a cathedral. The intermittent rain of the night before had died away, but icy drops still fell from the invisible tree-tops high above.

'Ready, sections?' whispered Lieutenant Narsing. 'The track's just visible. Follow it to the water, Six Section leading.'

In twenty minutes the leading scout halted. It was growing steadily lighter, and he signalled back to his section commander: 'Water just ahead!'

'Spread out and cross,' whispered Narsing. 'Spread out wide.'

'The camp, the enemy camp—it's just on the far side,' came the whisper back to him. 'It's empty. They've gone.'

The Gurkhas hastily splashed across the swift rocky stream and scattered to look for tracks.

'Count the sleeping places,' ordered Narsing, and in the growing light Manbahadur went round counting the impressions in the ground where Chinese had lain.

'I make it thirty-four,' he reported, 'and they camped before dark—they'd had time to cut these fan-shaped leaves to stick at an angle in the ground to keep the rain off.'

'H'm.' The officer nodded. 'Now, where's that boy Aitahang? Here, lad—how long have they been gone?'

Aitahang, ravenous and shivering in the damp mist, and soaked by the stream crossing, spent a few moments roaming the bivouac site and looking at the well-trampled trail which led beyond it, then answered, 'No more than half an hour. But, Huzoor'—he pointed to the track—'they didn't separate to leave the camp!'

'H'm.' Narsing rubbed his jaw thoughtfully. He looked around at the small groups of men awaiting his orders. He was puzzled. The Chinese must suspect that Gurkhas were still on their trail. Why did they not take the usual precaution of walking out separately from the night camp and meeting up several hundred yards away? But this time they had carelessly left together—why? But he was wasting time. There was only one thing to do, and that was to set off fast along the enemy tracks. 'Six Section!' he ordered. 'Lead off, but change your scout every ten minutes.' He had no need to remind them why.

Walking quietly with Four Section in the rear of the little column Aitahang had time to glance around him. That was good water just behind them—cold and clear from the rocky slopes above, swift-running and deep—but the roar of water that he heard last night came from higher up.

The terrorists' tracks led up along a rising ridge above the torrent, and as he climbed Aitahang remembered something Manbahadur had said the evening before and he nodded to himself in agreement; now in full daylight this high forest with its great trees and rushing torrents did indeed resemble the stretch of wooded hill across the Mewa from his home. He had a strange feeling of recognition; something seemed to be tugging him back in time, but he shook his head—he must keep his mind on the work ahead. Resolutely he tried to shut these persistent fancies out of his mind, and concentrated on keeping a sharp lookout around.

The Gurkhas climbed on with the noise of water growing louder, till some two hundred feet above the bivouac site the ridge levelled out at a false crest, broadening out for some yards before beginning to climb again. In front the leading scout stopped, looked up, then across to his left, and turned back to consult his section commander. 'What is it?' asked the platoon commander, and from below Aitahang saw the scout gesture across to the left. 'The trail turns across the hill-side!' whispered the men. The officer waved and the scout nodded, tucked his rifle under his arm once more and turned across the hill-side, and the others followed him in single file.

As he reached the false crest Aitahang's ears were struck by the roar of water and through the tree-trunks he glimpsed the head of the ravine farther on, where white water leapt over a rocky shelf to fall foaming into a pool fifty feet below. A mist of spray stood out from the falling water and he watched in sudden pleasure as a stray shaft of light touched it with rainbow colours—then he gasped aloud.

'Get a move on, lad,' grunted Kulbahadur behind him, but Aitahang did not notice. He stared all about him, his heart pounding in his chest. That brief rainbow spectrum, the noisy waterfall, the slope among the trees and the turn of the trail across the slope—all took him back, back years to a young boy leading his father and brother on the trail of a leopard. As he gulped in realization a door in his mind, long locked, seemed to open and he saw once again the massive shaven head of the Lama, and heard the sonorous warning, '. . . remember the leopard.'

He bounded forward and seized his section commander by the arm. 'Corporal!' he hissed through clenched teeth. 'Stop! We must stop at once!'

The section commander stared at him as if he had taken leave of his senses. In front the other sections plodded on steadily across the slope, and with a hiss of despair Aitahang flung away from Bhimbahadur and thrust hastily past the men in front till he reached the officer. 'Stop, Huzoor,' he said without ceremony, 'stop at once!'

Lieutenant Narsing clicked his tongue, the Gurkhas paused and heads turned curiously. 'What is it?' asked the platoon commander with a trace of impatience. 'We'll lose 'em if we don't keep on going.'

'We must stop, Huzoor—the terrorists are waiting for us.'

'How d'you know—isn't this still their main track?'

'It is their main track.'

'Have any turned off?'

'None have turned off so far—but ahead they have turned uphill and then back across the trail. They will ambush us as we walk past below them.'

Narsing stared at him. 'How can you know all this?' he demanded. He was beginning to think that the strain had turned the boy's mind, and sighed; they had lost precious minutes already. He ordered with rough kindness, 'Back to your place, lad—we've only a little more to do,' and was about to wave on the leading section when to his stupefaction Aitahang put out an arm to stop him. Such a thing had never happened to the officer before, and he was about to shake Aitahang roughly off when the young soldier, speaking urgently, said, 'Huzoor, my spirit tells me this,' and the officer lowered his arm and looked at him intently.

This was different, quite different. Behind the officer the expressions on the faces of the platoon sergeant and the signaller became grave.

'Tell me,' said Narsing.

'A waterfall, a hill, tracks across a slope—that is what I have been warned to look for,' said Aitahang. He did not explain further; it would have taken too long.

'And your spirit warns that they will be above the trail somewhere, waiting for us?'

'Yes, Huzoor!' confirmed Aitahang, once again the disciplined soldier.

'H'm.' Narsing Limbu looked about him, back towards the noisy waterfall, across the slope in the direction the trail led, and uphill above the trail. The hill-side curved round and the trail vanished out of sight among the trees. Everything seemed quiet; there were certainly no enemy immediately ahead; worriedly he visualized them striding out, and getting farther and farther away with every moment that he wasted listening to the wild fancy of a young lad overwrought through tiredness and hunger. And yet . . . why had the Chinese deliberately left a great trampled trail out of their bivouac? He glanced at Aitahang again, and the clear, calm and certain gaze in the boy's eyes decided him. He ordered, 'Section commanders!'

Rapidly he explained, and they nodded. Spiritual forces and the powers of good and evil were ever present in Gurkha thoughts, and the brief story of Aitahang's warning was accepted with immediate understanding.

'We must climb high,' said Lieutenant Narsing, 'and get above them. If we find them Six Section and Five Section will take cover while Four Section goes right round beyond to cut off their escape. When Four are in position Five and Six sections will close in very slowly and open up at close range. Got it?'

'They'll break away downhill,' commented Six Section commander.

'Very likely, but we just haven't enough men to cover every escape route. Now, any more questions?'

'Suppose we don't find anything,' said Bhimbahadur. 'How long do we search before starting to track 'em again?'

Narsing paused, glancing at his watch. 'It's ten past seven. If we don't find anything in twenty minutes we must assume that there's no ambush and that it is all a wild dream of the boy's. One last thing; stack packs here. We might as well do this unencumbered. The signaller will stay and open his set if we find something.' The sun was well up, and Narsing looked round his section commanders. 'We'll find out one way or the other before we're very much older. Off we go.'

When they had silently stacked their packs the Gurkhas began to climb up high above the line of trampled footprints. This was work they understood well and did to perfection—rapid, silent hill climbing with the aim of outflanking and annihilating an enemy and, tired and aching with hunger though they were, they moved up with astonishing speed. At length Narsing clicked his tongue, the leading scout glanced back and was waved across the slope again, and now with great care, they began to move across the steep, crumbly slope between the enormous trees. It was seven fifteen.

Slowly the minutes passed as the Gurkhas patiently worked their way round the curving flank of the hill. Every man was now on the lookout for the enemy expected below, as well as glancing above them—just in case—but the minutes ticked by and more and more of the slope below them was seen to be empty. Then they reached a point where the hill fissured into another but smaller ravine with another fast stream in it, and Narsing shook his head. There was still no sign of the enemy. He looked at his watch and clicked his tongue to recall the leading section. It was seven twenty-seven.

A little way behind him Aitahang stood desolate. He had, it seemed, finally lost the platoon its chance of catching up with the enemy. He felt torn between the instinct to remain silent, to admit that his warning had been wrong—and the even stronger conviction that the Lama was right. Aitahang *knew* he was right! The enemy *were* waiting somewhere ahead. He set his teeth: he would tackle the platoon commander once more. Doggedly he went up to him and blurted out, 'Huzoor—let me go on a little,' then words failed him and he stood with lowered head, waiting for the angry reprimand.

But Narsing himself was beginning to have certain suspicions, and once again thought back to that all-too-obvious trail out from the enemy camp. He looked at his watch again. It was now seven twenty-eight—but he had said the search would go on till seven thirty. He nodded, and said briefly, 'Two minutes.'

Aitahang slipped past the sections in front and, moving as fast and silently as he knew how, slithered down the flank of the ravine, sprang lightly from rock to rock across the foaming water and scrambled up the far side. At the topmost edge he raised his head very slowly, and saw beyond and below only the trampled foot-prints running along beside a line of rocks edging a gap in the big trees. He began to pull himself up over the edge—then eased himself back down again. His eye had caught a slight movement, a barely perceptible shift of a trouser-leg behind a tree. He held his breath. They were there! Crouching there he studied the ground and, one by one picked out outlines of men lying hidden, some behind trees, others behind clumps of rock. He could see a dozen, fairly well spread out above the trail, and he reckoned there were many more lying out of sight.

He sank below the lip of the ravine and turned his head. On the far side Narsing stood watching. He knew the boy had seen something, and at Aitahang's gesture he waved back and brought the remainder across the torrent and up to the far side. 'Where, boy?' he whispered, and Aitahang breathed into his ear, 'Ahead and below, waiting.'

The officer looked cautiously then brought up the section commanders. 'They're there all right,' he whispered, and added, 'Same plan—Four Section get right round the far side. Take it slowly, the rest of us'll move in in ten minutes.'

Exhaustion and hunger forgotten, Four Section worked their way along beneath the lip of the ravine to get still higher before crossing the slope above the enemy position. With his section once again was Aitahang, and Bhimbahadur had just time for a hasty 'Well done' before leading off.

In the ten minutes of waiting the others felt their ammunition pouches, checked that clips and magazines were ready, and for the dozenth time felt their safety catches. Narsing lay peering down at the enemy and thinking. From behind him the roar of the waterfall sounded in his ears, and he was puzzled. Chinese terrorists seldom paused in position near noisy water—they liked to be able to hear every leaf-rustle by an approaching Gurkha. Yet, although the bandit commander knew this area like the back of his hand, he had chosen this particular point. But there was nothing to be gained by puzzling that out now. He glanced at his watch: two minutes to go.

Screened from the Chinese by intervening trees Four Section worked their way across the slope till Bhimbahadur estimated that they were a good sixty yards beyond the end of the ambush position, then he led his little group downhill to a point roughly level with it. He looked around for a moment or two, then placed out his men—himself, Kesersing and Kulbahadur with the bren in the centre, Bombahadur several yards higher uphill, and Aitahang well down the slope. 'They may turn down this way when they meet the bren,' he whispered, 'you should get a shot or two. You're on your own down here, but just take it steady,' and with an encouraging pat on the shoulder he left Aitahang to make himself secure behind a tree.

From where he crouched Aitahang could see no enemy at all, only thickets of trees on the slope, and the near end of that unusual bare fringe of rock. It was difficult to see clearly, but there seemed to be some sort of gap downhill from it. He looked round again, still saw no movement and again looked curiously at the rock fringe. There seemed to be an empty space below it, as if there were a giant step in the slope. He stared harder. There *was* an empty space, and below it only tree-tops. He gave a low hiss of comprehension: that rock ledge was the upper edge of a precipice. No wonder the terrorists had chosen this as their ambush position! With light machine-guns on one side and a death-fall on the other not one soldier would have escaped.

Aitahang felt his heart begin to thud. This was One-Eye's

work all right; it had the same touch of merciless finality about it that had characterized the road ambush. 'Steady,' he told himself. 'Keep calm, don't throw everything away by getting excited at *this* stage, when One-Eye must be so close.' He took a long, shaky breath and felt his heartbeats slow down a little. That was better. He breathed deeply and thought, 'Any minute now . . .' and ahead the first rifle-shot exploded.

Although he could not see the Chinese, Aitahang could almost feel their shocked, appalled surprise. There was confused movement and he caught a brief glimpse of khaki-uniformed men scrambling desperately round to face uphill, then a storm of rifle and automatic fire burst down on them from a half-ring of bright muzzle-flashes. Shattered branches, leaves and bark fell and mingled with showers of churned-up earth, ricochets spun buzzing from the rocks, the noise was deafening, and to Aitahang it seemed that nothing could survive that bullet-storm. Yet from the ambush position sporadic bursts of bren and tommy-gun fire began to answer back. A Gurkha in olive-green fell from behind his tree and was shot again and again as he tumbled downhill. Aitahang caught no more than a glimpse of him, for in front two khaki-clad figures came scuttling through the trees towards them, looking up towards the Gurkhas on the slope above.

'Right, bren-gunner!' Bhimbahadur struck Kulbahadur on the shoulder, he fired two short bursts and the two men collapsed—but in a moment the bren group themselves came under a hail of fire and dived for cover.

Still undiscovered down the slope Aitahang could only guess at the havoc caused by the two sections above. But it was also clear that a good number of the enemy were still alive and fighting back ferociously. With the precipice behind them they had two alternatives—to stay and fight it out to the death or try and break through the Gurkha ring. From the slope above, the Gurkhas, firing and moving, were gradually closing in on the Chinese. Looking up Aitahang caught a glimpse of one Gurkha step out from behind a tree, his arm swung and something small and black went spinning down into the Chinese positions. There was a sharp explosion and the whing of fragments, agonized cries and the shooting from the Chinese positions dwindled abruptly. Another grenade hurtled down and its detonation was followed by a babble of groans and shouts, a loud command in Chinese and a roar from Bhimbahadur, 'Here they come!' as the surviving Chinese made a rush to escape.

In a moment the trees in front of Four Section seemed full of men. Kulbahadur heaved his bren gun to his hip and fired burst after burst into them, the Chinese rush disintegrated and running, stumbling men broke left and right. From below, Aitahang fired and reloaded, fired and reloaded. One man fell in front of him; another, clutching an M1 carbine, blundered down almost into him. Aitahang fired into him at point-blank range and he dropped his weapon and staggered away downhill with great unsteady strides, clutching his chest with both hands. Aitahang worked his bolt—but his rifle was empty, and he snatched at his pouch for another clip of ammunition.

Just for a moment there was one of those curious lulls that happen in close-quarter battles, with the first initial shock over, numbers dead or wounded and the survivors reloading and trying to see what was happening. As he fumbled in his pouch Aitahang tried to clear his throat, but could not; his mouth and throat were dry and parched with excitement, and his left ear sang from the muzzle-blast of the bren. Everywhere there seemed to be bodies —most in light khaki, but farther uphill one or two in olive-green. Chest-high among the trees hung a layer of blue smoke, with wisps drifting away, and through it the nearest men of Five Section were moving down towards the ambush position. So much he saw in one hasty glance round when the lull was broken by scattered shots, the quick high-pitched rip of tommy-gun fire and shouts of 'Watch out! More coming!'

Behind his tree Aitahang was hurriedly reloading. He pushed the clip down into the breech charger guide, but his thumb slipped forward on the oily rounds and the nose of the top round jammed in the breech at an angle. As he wrestled with it shots exploded above him and bullets cracked across his front. Anxiously he looked round his tree. A Chinese in khaki with another some distance behind him was running and ducking through the trees at an angle towards him—a Chinese holding a Luger automatic; a lean man with a bony face, who ran with his head cocked slightly to one side, the better to see with his single remaining eye. It was One-Eye, and Aitahang faced him with a jammed and useless rifle. In a moment or two he would be past and down into the trees below, escaped once more.

Swinging his rifle like a club Aitahang sprang out at him, but One-Eye swerved away, twisting his body so that the rifle butt no more than grazed his temple. Unbalanced by the violence of his swing Aitahang staggered, and the Chinese raised his Luger, took aim and fired twice into the young Gurkha. Aitahang felt a burning pain score along the side of his neck and a hammer-blow in his left shoulder, and his left arm dropped uselessly at his side. Seeing his enemy turn to get away he grabbed the rifle with his right arm and thrust it between One-Eye's legs, and the terrorist tripped and went sprawling down the slope with Aitahang after him.

He raised his Luger as he scrambled up and Aitahang snatched out his kukri and with a backhand slash cut through One-Eye's fingers and the Luger fell to the ground. As One-Eye gaped helplessly at the bleeding stumps of his fingers Aitahang swung up the kukri and brought it down with the last of his strength, chopping deeply into the unprotected angle between head and neck. His chest cut nearly in half, One-Eye collapsed, and the kukri was wrenched from Aitahang's hand in his fall.

He stooped to recover it—just as a burst of bullets crackled where his head had been, and he looked up to see the terrorist behind, a short, thick-set Chinese with a tommy-gun. Weak and bleeding Aitahang scrabbled for the Luger, the Chinese lifted his tommy-gun again, a rifle banged close by and he was knocked off balance by a bullet which struck him in the ribs under the right arm, a bullet fired from a short distance higher up the slope by Manbahadur. The terrorist, wounded and staggering, tried to turn to swing up his weapon but Manbahadur sprang down at him and shot him at point-blank range, saw him fall dead and rushed to where Aitahang sat beside the body of One-Eye.

'We all saw it as we charged down, Aitey—what a wonderful blow! But here,' and Manbahadur eased his friend gently down, 'you've been hit pretty hard. Let's have a look.' His eyes narrowed at the two bullet wounds, but he said reassuringly, 'Everything's going to be all right—the fight's over, and we've won.'

He was busy tearing open Aitahang's field-dressing pocket when his glance fell on the dreadful corpse with the long kukri buried in its chest. 'Here, I'll get your kukri,' he said, adding in surprise as he recognized the buffalo-horn handle. 'It's your good one!' He put a foot on the corpse to help pull it out when his glance rested for a moment on the dead face with its open mouth, the gold teeth exposed in a terrible grimace and the solitary staring eye focused on the tree-tops high above. 'It's One-Eye!' he breathed, almost in disbelief. 'One-Eye—and you killed him with your own hand!' He pulled out the kukri, wiped it clean on One-Eye's trousers and slid it back into Aitahang's scabbard. 'There you are! Now we'll get you properly tied up!'

Hurrying down the slope came Corporal Bhimbahadur with the section medical pack. 'Use shell dressings,' he ordered, 'they're bigger.' While Manbahadur put a pillow of rolled up shirt and haversack under Aitahang's head the section commander deftly and efficiently checked the flow of blood, padded the wounds with shell dressings, put Aitahang's left arm in a sling and bound it close to his body with windings of bandage so that it would not move. Finally he said, 'Morphia,' and injected a syrette of colourless fluid into the boy's right arm. 'There, now; just take it easy. We'll get you out of this in no time.'

Very pale, Aitahang muttered 'Water', and Manbahadur took out his water-bottle and unscrewed the top.

'Only a little, now,' warned Bhimbahadur. 'Too much water after morphia and he'll be sick.' He thought back to the last time he himself had been wounded, how he had gulped water and vomited it all up again. He turned at a movement. It was the platoon commander, pistol in hand, his webbing equipment torn by bullets and a bloody field dressing binding his scalp. 'How's the lad?'

'Hit hard.' Bhimbahadur spoke in a low voice.

'That's bad,' replied Narsing, also speaking low. 'He looks as if he's lost some blood. We must get him back as fast as we can.' He looked at his watch. It was just after eight. 'Shouldn't be too long before the others catch up. Look after the boy.' He nodded and moved off to continue his tour of the battlefield but turned back briefly. 'It's through *him* that we're not laid out like that lot,' and he nodded to where the surviving Gurkhas were dragging the dead terrorists into a rough heap to be counted.

'Some got away,' commented Bhimbahadur in a matter-of-fact tone.

'Not many—and they won't bother anyone for a long time.'

'What about our own casualties, Sahib?'

'One dead in Six Section; two wounded in Five.'

'And yourself, Sahib.'

'It's nothing much—didn't know I'd been hit till the platoon runner told me.'

The platoon sergeant called down, 'There are two wounded Chinese here.'

'Watch 'em,' came warning shouts, 'don't let them grenade you!'

'Not them, they're too sorry for themselves!' The wounded terrorists lay white and silent. 'Come on, we'll bandage them up.'

The fury of the fight had buoyed up the men of Four Platoon, but now that it was over they sat exhausted. Narsing looked about him. Less than half of the Benom gang had managed to break away during the fighting. They would now be scattered—some to their base camp, others to hide with sympathizers in the villages around Kuala Krau on the railway line. He should have every man out now, trying to pick up tracks so that pursuit could be mounted—but first they must have a moment's rest. Slowly and wearily he sat down.

There was a movement back along the trail and a shout or two. He pushed himself up. 'What is it?'

'It's the Major Sahib, and the rest of the company.'

# 14 THE LAST DANGER

The commander of the Recruiting Depot leaned back in his chair thoughtfully studying a letter in his hand. Far across the valley behind his window broken cloud scudded across the glaciers of Kangchenjunga and swirled round the ice-peaks on either side, but he did not spare a glance at them, for the letter intrigued him. It was laconic enough, merely mentioning that a certain soldier recovering from wounds had been granted 90 days' sick leave together with 28 days' annual leave, plus the appropriate travelling and ration allowances for the journey home to Mewa Khola. What interested him was that this was not the normal leave season, and the soldier's name, he glanced down at the letter—oh yes,

Aitahang Limbu—was familiar. He pondered a moment, then nodded. He remembered now.

'Stick Orderly!' he called.

Outside the glass-paned office door a Gurkha soldier with a silver-topped cane under his arm snapped to attention, entered the office and saluted. 'Huzoor!'

'Tell the 10th Gurkha Captain Sahib that I will see that leave man now,' he ordered in curt Gurkhali, and a few moments later a middle-aged Gurkha Captain with three rows of ribbons on his massive chest came in, saluted and said in a jovial wheezy tone, 'I've got the lad here, Sahib—shall I bring him in?'

'Yes, please, Captain Sahib—but first, how is he, fit to travel?'

'So he says, Sahib, but you know these boys when they're on their way home—they'd tell you anything.'

'Has the doctor had a look at him?'

'He has—seems surprised he survived.' His jovial tone became serious. 'Aitahang's one of these very quiet ones, Sahib—you know . . .' he paused a moment, 'more mind than body. Anyway, you have a word with him—*I'm* not making much impression!' He chuckled, then straightened his face, turned and jerked his head at the soldier standing stiffly to attention facing the glass-paned door. The Stick Orderly threw the door open, the soldier marched in, halted, turned with a sharp click of boot-heels and saluted. 'Twenty-two Thirteen Sixty-Six Thirteen Rifleman Aitahang Limbu, Sahib!' announced the Captain with an impeccable salute.

Once more the Depot Commander leaned back in his chair, this time studying the young soldier standing motionless in front of him. He remembered, all right—the papers had been full of this exploit. He had many years of service with the Gurkhas, much of it on operations of one sort or another, yet he never ceased to feel surprise at the contrast between the quiet, impassive, even placid demeanour of the Gurkha soldier on parade, or at rest or on the march, and the immediate transformation to ferocity in battle. And this lad here, obviously younger than his stated age (how had he managed to get enlisted? 'What could I have been thinking about?') had, according to the papers, been the hero of a savage battle at close quarters against much greater numbers. All too often newspapers got things wrong, but this time their reports were correct enough and, he remembered, the lad had been decorated for his exploit—his second medal for gallantry.

'I congratulate you on your decorations,' he said gravely, and

Aitahang gave a brief, embarrassed half-cough. 'Wounds healing well?'

'Huzoor!' affirmed Aitahang.

'H'm.' The Depot Commander half-turned and glanced briefly out of the window before turning back again. 'You are going home on leave—' He looked up at the Gurkha Captain. 'Anyone else going up to Taplejung, Sahib?'

The Gurkha officer shook his head. 'No one, Sahib—we've no leave men at all now, the last small batch left two weeks ago, and I don't think we'll see anyone for a bit.'

The Depot Commander looked at Aitahang. 'You understand what he means? I'd rather you didn't cross that frontier section alone. Will you wait? There might well be some leave man arriving who can travel with you.'

'Sahib,' replied Aitahang, 'the monsoon is about to break.'

The Depot Commander turned again and glanced at Kangchenjunga. What from here looked like gently waving lace was, he knew, a freezing hell of icy cloud. In a day or two it would thicken and spread out and sink, rain would burst downwards from it and slash at the Gurkha hills, and the trickling stream-beds would turn in a flash to raging torrents—torrents which would sweep away men to their deaths among flying spray and tumbling rocks. The young soldier was right—he either left now or waited for weeks. The Depot Commander nodded: 'Very well, but at least we can get you on your way as quickly as possible.' He looked up at the Gurkha officer. 'Captain Sahib, see that Aitahang gets his pay, savings deposit and allowances straight away. Has he had morning khana?'

'Ji, Sahib,' nodded the Captain.

'Right. As soon as he's been paid and his documents completed get the M.T.O. Sahib to put him in a Land Rover and send him as far as Daragaon. He can then have a straight climb up to Phalut—it'll be a bit quicker than doing the walk from the end of the road at Budhbari.'

'*Hunchha*, Sahib,' acknowledged the Gurkha officer, 'it shall be done. And from Phalut he'll be safe in Gurkha territory.'

'Good. And now, Aitahang, remember not to strain your wounds getting home *too* quickly! Off you go.' He acknowledged the soldier's salute with a brief nod of the head and turned back to study the first of the next problems awaiting his attention—this time a soldier's request for help over a land dispute.

In the meantime Aitahang was changing out of his uniform—the uniform of a foreign army, as far as Nepal was concerned—into hillman's smock and jodhpurs. Round his waist he wound his patuka, the broad white cummerbund, and into it he thrust his Limbu kukri. On his head he perched the hillman's pointed skull-cap, round his neck he hung a warm woollen scarf of bright colours knitted for sale in the Depot by the wife of a pensioner. On his feet he wore a pair of new rubber-soled jungle boots, and over his shoulder he slung a standard webbing haversack. In it he carried carefully packed a group photograph of his company, his money in a bundle of 10-rupee notes (ready to pay the old Phedangba) and, almost as precious, the cases with the two heavy silver discs of the Military Medal and the Distinguished Conduct Medal, presented him only two weeks before by the Commander-in-Chief in person. Rammed in on top was a lightweight jungle blanket, and the whole was bound into a compact bundle by a length of parachute cord. His uniform and leather boots he packed neatly into a kitbag and handed in to the Depot store for collection on his return.

From the road above the store a driver called down, 'Leave wallah—going?'

'Going, Huzoor,' called Aitahang eagerly and scrambled up the bank and climbed in beside the driver with his precious haversack clasped close; they started up and drove off down to the main road, turned down through Darjeeling and then off west, in an hour they were at Daragaon and Aitahang was jumping out. 'Lau, Huzoor,' he said in polite acknowledgement to the driver, an older soldier with many ribbons and therefore entitled to respect, even from new young heroes.

'Take it steady now,' warned the older man, 'you'll make it all right before the monsoon.' He waved, backed and turned and drove off. Aitahang slung his haversack a little closer, took a deep breath and looked about him. It seemed an age since he first came down through Daragaon with his recruiter, yet it was less than two years. The border village looked unchanged—the same short row of shops, the same dusty street, the same bunch of loafers chewing betel-nut and spitting, even the same big fellow—still idling. But that was nothing to do with Aitahang; all he had to do was set off up that high steep climb to the Phalut ridge, some 5,000 feet above him. As he looked up at the mountain slope, reckoning whether he'd make the ridge that night, a voice called, 'Oho, soldier—' and he turned. It was one of the goldsmiths, squatting at the front of his shop with his little iron tools spread before him and the crucible and charcoal fire glowing behind him. 'Soldier,' he called again, 'buy gold to take home with you—your wife will want ornaments made up for her.'

'No wife yet,' Aitahang replied briefly and began to move away, annoyed at the attention the man was drawing to him, but the goldsmith went on persuasively, 'well, if not for a wife, use the gold for land—and if not for land you can keep it, buried, it won't rot like paper money, it's easily hidden, no one will know . . .' He delved behind him and held up something small. 'See, gold takes up little space!' It was a small bar of the yellow metal, no more than two inches long and a quarter of an inch thick. 'I will sell you these, and you can carry them easily. And,' he went on, 'they won't spoil with the monsoon damp—' He stopped and lowered his hand. Aitahang was striding off, determined to get out of that delaying village and up on to the track up to the border ridge—called Phalut on this side and Phalelung on the other.

He strode out, ignoring the glances and murmured comments of the loafers leaning against a wall of one of the shops. As he passed it he wrinkled his nostrils at the drifting odour of rice-spirit mingling with the bitter scent of Tibetan barley beer and the more flavoursome smells of rice and meat cooking. In spite of himself he paused at the next shop, however, for displayed were bolts of coloured cotton cloth and one of dark blue velvet. He could spare five minutes to buy a few yards of *that* for his mother and sister! He did not spend long haggling over the price, only regretting that he had been able to spend no time in the wonderful bazaars of Darjeeling: out here things were a terrible price. He chose quickly, paid for it with some of the money carried separately in his pocket and pushed his purchase into his haversack, under his blanket.

As he swung his haversack on again the shopkeeper, an ox-eyed Newar, said, 'It is past midday, soldier, will you cross the mountain by dark? Why not stay a night here and leave at dawn?'

Aitahang shook his head. The shopkeeper meant well, but his advice was not very practical. 'Thank you,' he replied politely, 'but I have far to go.'

'Whither?' asked the Newar, and at the answer 'Mewa Khola', nodded his head. 'I have not been there, but I know from travellers that it is distant. You are a Limbu?'

'I am a Limbu,' confirmed Aitahang.

'May Ram and Shiva watch over your journey,' said the Newar, and Aitahang gave him a quick smile of thanks, noting with some relief as he left that the rather unpleasant-looking little group of loafers had disappeared.

The path outside the village straggled through one or two small-holdings where tethered buffaloes grazed. Nepalis in ragged peasant dress padded past him bearing great loads of cut firewood with the namlo, not giving him a glance. Young men returning from the wars were a common enough sight on the borders of Nepal.

Beyond the small-holdings and their still-dry terraced fields the path wound upwards, at first through eroded gullies and rocky ground, then abruptly vanishing into the wild mixed jungle that ran to within a thousand feet of the Phalut ridge high above. Aitahang stepped out confidently, gripping the sling of his haversack, and as he entered the shade of the trees he smiled faintly to himself. He hadn't been in among trees since he'd been carried out of the forest beyond Karak. His mind was full of excited thoughts—of the land, of Bhalu the dog, the flock and the cattle, his family's astonishment—for his leave had been awarded so suddenly there had been no chance to send a letter on ahead—the surprise and joy would be wonderful.

He climbed vigorously uphill, lost in his thoughts, and it was only after he had covered a good mile of steep rocky path that he reminded himself that he was walking alone through woods on the wrong side of the border. Surely this knowledge was the reason for his growing sense of uneasiness, almost, he grimaced, as if there were Chinese terrorists moving in to ambush him. He shook his head in annoyance: there were no Chinese here! He strode on determinedly but the feeling of unease increased. He slowed down a little and his gaze fastened on a group of boulders above and to one side of the path. He paused, there was movement there—but there was movement behind him as well, twigs snapped, he caught a whiff of panting breath close to him and as he snatched out his kukri something smashed against the side of his head. As he sank down feet came running up, more blows rained down on him and as he collapsed unconscious on the path his half-healed neck wound opened and blood rushed out. 'You've killed him, you fool!' said an agitated voice. 'I told you we were doing this too close in!'

'Ah, don't worry—we didn't have much time.' The speaker was rolling Aitahang over and prising the kukri loose from his clenched fingers. 'Another Limbu, by the look of this kukri. Here, I'll take the haversack. Now, let's clear off.'

'But if he's dead—'

'Dead men don't complain,' grunted the other. 'We'll dump him in the jungle well off the path. Either the jackals will clean him up or the birds will. In any case, by the time he's found no one'll know what had happened. He could have slipped on those rocks.'

'And then walked into the jungle to die?' asked the other sarcastically.

'You worry too much,' said the first man roughly. 'Grab his feet.' Together, half-carrying and half-dragging the young soldier they pushed their way off the path and through the tangle of vegetation between the trees. Thirty yards in the two robbers let him drop, and raked up twigs and leaves to cover him. 'There,' said the first man, 'no one'll ever find him. Now, let's get back separately to Daragaon. Meet you at the *raksi-khana* this evening about sundown. We'll share out there.'

'What about here and now!' demanded the other.

'There's only my bag here—it'll all have to go in that for now; we daren't be seen carrying this army haversack. Don't worry—I won't take any of it! Now,' he said hurriedly, 'we must get off the track and go back carefully; it'll take us till evening to get down through this thick stuff. We'd better not be seen on the path.'

After a while a small bird, attracted by the smell of drying blood from the motionless hump under the leaves, glided down, then flew off again in alarm at a slight movement. Nothing happened for several moments while the bird watched from a branch then, when it was about to investigate once more, the leaf covering was disturbed, an arm moved, there was a murmur, another long interval of silence and then Aitahang lifted his arm and brushed away the leaves over his face. His fingers felt sticky and he gazed at the blood on them, only half-comprehending. Cautiously he felt his head and neck; they were sticky with blood, but the wound had stopped bleeding. But he now located the pain which made him feel so sick and weak; a huge bump above his right ear ached and throbbed. The skin had been broken and he felt the stickiness of blood there as well.

For some minutes longer he lay there, feeling helpless and

betrayed. Mechanically he felt for his kukri, but it had gone, and he knew that his haversack had gone as well. What he had been warned against had happened, and he was only lucky to be still alive. But in his present state of mind that was no consolation—his mental anguish was far greater than the throbbing pain in his head and the aches from the bruises where he had been beaten about the body. How could he go home empty-handed—a failure? He would be shamed for life. In spite of himself tears of pain and weakness and frustration trickled from his eyes, cleaning warm furrows through the blood on his face, and he groaned in shame. He had not wept since he was eight years old.

But it was this same sense of shame that made him set his teeth and struggle up into a sitting position. Shame was goading him into defying his weakness, his battered head and his reopened wound. He had to do something—anything. He could not just meekly accept the loss of his savings, his kukri, his medals, even the little presents of velvet. How he would go about trying to recover them he had not the faintest idea; here in this enormous border area with its scattered villages, numerous travellers and mixed population, how would he ever find the men who had beaten him down and robbed him? They would be far away by now, and he had not even caught a glimpse of them.

He sat with his head in his hands, trying to collect his thoughts and remember what had happened. Gradually he recalled his feelings of unease, his suspicion of the rocks ahead, the rustle behind him, the panting breath—there he checked his thoughts. He hadn't seen the man behind him, but he'd smelt him, a mingling of familiar smells—tobacco and rice-spirit, the rice-spirit strongest. And he himself had unwisely lingered to buy velvet from the Newar just beyond that grog-shop.

He pushed himself up on to his hands and knees while the pain stabbed at his head. He retched a moment, feeling sick and shaky, then cold anger took charge. He knew who had done it—those loafers; most probably the big one and a couple of others. Aitahang stood upright, brushed off some of the leaves and twigs and glanced about him. Very quickly he saw the drag marks where he had been pulled and carried, and followed them back to the path. On the earth near the beaten path he studied the ground very carefully, almost more carefully than in his search for the leopard, or later for One-Eye. Soon he was able to confirm his original suspicions: there had been two men, both wearing leather shoes, one man large and heavy, his prints deep, while the other was smaller and lighter. And on the ground a few yards down the path was a dirty red splash of betel-nut juice. There was no need to look further: he remembered the big fellow, he was the one to go for; and the place to find him was the grog-shop.

The sun had crossed the ridge and the shadows were deepening when Aitahang reached the terraced fields above the village. Instead of entering it he circled round, keeping to the fringe of the scrub jungle. He would achieve nothing by walking in—the robbers would spot him and would vanish again, hiding their booty, and he would never recover it. No, he must surprise them—but dealing with them would be no easy task, for he had no weapon and physically was no match for anyone at the moment, let alone a big man armed with a club and possibly Aitahang's own kukri.

He thought hard, studying the untidy roofs of the village shops in the weakening light. He tried to identify the grog-shop, and noticed one backyard rather larger than the others, more or less where he estimated that it should be, with two or three large chili-bushes growing in it, and smaller bushes of other herbs—just what an inn-keeper would need to spice the meals he served to travellers. As he watched, Aitahang saw the glimmer of lamps; evening was here and soon it would be quite dark, and he did not yet know what to do. Instinctively he crept out and across the empty terraced fields and settled in a corner and, as soon as it was dark enough, crept into the yard behind the grog-shop. For some minutes he waited while the darkness closed down, till the only light in the yard was that cast by a lamp in the back window of the grog-shop. With the dark the temperature began to fall and Aitahang shivered in the growing cold, but he gave it no thought; from the grog-shop he heard voices, and he crept up to the window and looked in.

At the far end, nearest the street, men in hill dress sat drinking at a table. To Aitahang's right opened the kitchen, the reek of hot barley beer coming from it, with one or two people moving about by the light of the kitchen fire and a hurricane lamp. But at a small table set inconspicuously near the very window through which he peered, two men sat facing each other, not speaking, but occasionally glancing round casually as if to see whether they were being observed. The man seated facing the rear window was small, and Aitahang remembered him as one of the small knot of loafers he had seen earlier in the day. But with his back to Aitahang sat a big man, hunched over the table and with some sort of bag or bundle tucked carefully between himself and the wall.

Even from behind Aitahang recognized the big man, but now that he was so close to him he felt a pang of doubt. *Was* this the robber? Would he just sit there calmly knowing that his victim might return to look for him? Then Aitahang thought of the leaves which had covered him. Whoever had robbed him had left him for dead.

Even so, the small doubt stuck in his mind. He strained his eyes trying to get a look at the bundle beside the big man, but could only see the rough shape of it. It might have been an army haversack—then again, it might have just been one of the ordinary ornamented cloth bags so often carried over the shoulder by travellers. But these two did not look entirely at ease, continually looking round, and Aitahang clenched his teeth. He couldn't go on just wondering whether this was the man; he must decide. As he gazed at him the big man turned his head and spat a scarlet stream of betel-nut juice on to the earth floor. That decided him.

But, what could he do about it? If he went in and challenged him he might be roughly handled, perhaps killed, by the man and any of his friends. Neither could he sneak in and lift away the bag; it was being too carefully watched.

He stepped softly back from the window, crouched and felt about near the roots of a chili-bush till his hand closed on a stone. It was about the size of an apple, and fitted comfortably into the palm of his hand. He crept up the steps to the back door of the grog-shop, unlatched it gently and stepped inside. There was a certain amount of coming and going, together with the activity in the kitchen, and neither of the two men at the table looked up. Aitahang walked over to behind the big man, and the small man glanced up and his jaw dropped at the blood-smeared face before him. With all his strength Aitahang smashed the stone against the side of the big man's head, just above his right ear. He collapsed forward across the table, sending a bowlful of rice-spirit splashing against the small man, who started to get up just as Aitahang swung the stone again and buffeted him between the eyes. Then he flung down the stone, snatched up the bundle and sprang out through the door.

After a first startled silence uproar broke out, with shouts of 'Murder!', 'Thief!' and 'All out—hunt the thief!' Lights flared along the street and as he stumbled across the dry paddy fields in the darkness Aitahang heard the menacing shouts of a gathering crowd, drunken, ugly shouts, then at last he reached the edge of the jungle. For the moment, at least, he was safe, but he knew he must put as much ground between himself and the village as possible, in case he was cut off before he reached the Phalut ridge. But had those two been the robbers—or was he himself a robber? His hand explored the shape of the bundle he had snatched up, and his heart sank. He could not feel the hard webbing of a military haversack, nor were there buckles and straps. Instead he felt a softer, embroidered material, ornamented with decorative fringes. It was an ordinary traveller's bag, with ordinary traveller's goods inside it. He began to feel rather sick. He had attacked the wrong man.

His first instinct was to throw the bag away as a useless encumbrance, then he restrained himself. The bag was heavy, and the man—loafer or not—could hardly afford to lose the contents. No, he would carry it with him, and when he reached the path he'd put it down. Someone would pick it up, and would very likely drop it in at the police post at Tanglu or Budhbari. Most travellers were honest. The thought gave him a pang of despair. Not only had he let himself be robbed, but he himself had become a robber, and unless he got away quickly he'd be hunted down by the locals and the border police. Setting his teeth he began the long climb up through the dark jungle to the ridge.

Near midnight he stumbled across the path. He had meant to keep away from it, but now he saw that unless he followed the path he could not reach the ridge before morning, the going was far too difficult. He was far above the village by now, and he guessed that the men who had howled for his blood hours before would have felt little enthusiasm for setting ambushes all night in the cold on the off-chance of catching someone who might well have gone the opposite way. He sat down to listen but got up again at once. He was falling asleep. Unless he kept moving he was finished.

Slowly and painfully he climbed the path, forcing himself on by will-power and the thought of the danger behind, and by the first paling of the dark made out the hard line of the crest not far above. He struggled on, knowing that over the ridge lay safety, and by the time the light had strengthened enough for him to see he was climbing the last few yards to the crest. He paused, listened, and went up very slowly.

The crest line was empty. He had reached it first, and the track into Limbuan was before him. He had only one thought now, to get down on to the ridge above the Kabeli, turn aside at the first stream and drink and drink the icy water, then sleep till midday. He began to go over the crest, then paused with a muttered exclamation of annoyance. He had instinctively clung on to the bag all through the weary climb up, when he could have put it down on the path at midnight. He cursed his stupidity; he must have been hit harder than he thought.

All this time the light was strengthening. He looked round for a conspicuous spot on which to leave the bag. It was certainly heavy —*very* heavy to be carried about by a man who presumably lived in or near that village.

Aitahang felt inside. There seemed to be just the usual bundle of assorted oddments inside a cloth wrapping—but his fingers met material that felt familiar. He felt it more carefully. It was velvet. He opened the bag, shook out the bundled-up contents out on to the path and undid the cotton wrapping. Inside was a grey-blue lightweight blanket. He opened it out. There lay his kukri, his roll of ten-rupee notes, untouched, and the two crown-embossed white cardboard boxes. He opened them, and there were the heavy silver discs of his Military Medal and his Distinguished Conduct Medal. Carefully he repacked the bag, and slung it from his shoulder.

Behind him the sun was rising, and on the snow peaks the light shone grey, then pink, then purest white. On his right towered Kangchenjunga but before him to the north-west he saw, just short of the Great Himal where the Gods lived, his very own peak of Topke. With the wind from the Gurkha hills blowing in his face he set off over the ridge for home.

# GLOSSARY

*Gurkhali*

| | |
|---|---|
| AYO GURKHA! | The Gurkha comes! |
| DOKO | Large cone-shaped load-carrying basket |
| GALLA | Party of recruits |
| HIN! | March! |
| HUNCHHA! | Very well! |
| KONRA | Broad-headed forward-curving Gurkha sword |
| PUJA | Religious ceremony, prayer |
| RAKSI | Spirits |
| RAKSI-KHANA | Grog-shop |
| SHIKAR | Game, the hunt |

*Malay*

| | |
|---|---|
| BELUKAR | Dense secondary jungle |
| BESAR | Great, or large |
| BUKIT | Hill |
| ENCHE | Term of respect |
| GAJAH | Elephant |
| GUNONG | Mountain |
| HARI | Day |
| JALAN | Road |
| KAMPONG | Village |
| SELAMAT! | Greetings |
| SUNGEI | River or stream |

*Abbreviations*

| | |
|---|---|
| B.M.H. | British Military Hospital |
| C.T. | Communist terrorist |
| T.S.M.G. | Thompson sub-machine-gun |